The YORKSHIRE VET

In the footsteps of Herriot

PETER WRIGHT
Foreword by Jim Wight

Mirror Books

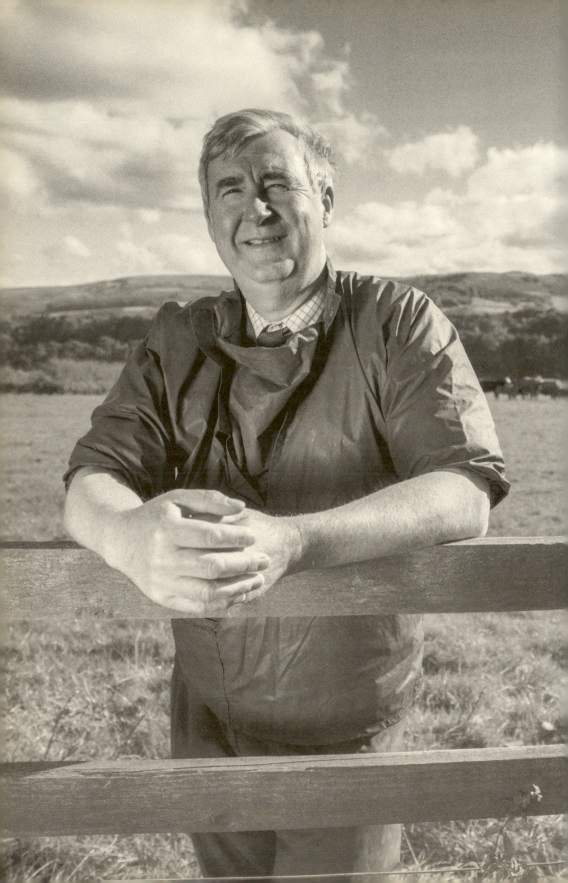

I'd like to dedicate this book
to my long-suffering wife Lin,
to whom I owe everything.

PETER WRIGHT

THE YORKSHIRE VET
by Peter Wright
with Helen Leavey

This book first published in 2018 by Mirror Books

Mirror Books is part of Reach plc
One Canada Square,
London E14 5AP,
England

www.mirrorbooks.co.uk

ISBN 978-1-9126-2411-9

5 7 9 10 8 6 4

First hardback edition 2018

Every effort has been made to fulfil requirements with regard to
reproducing copyright material. The author and publisher will be
glad to rectify any omissions at the earliest opportunity.

Cover: Cristian Barnett, iStockphoto
Plates: Cristian Barnett, Paul Gay/Daisybeck, courtesy of Peter Wright

CONTENTS

Jim out walking with his dog, Cleo.

FOREWORD
by Jim Wight

Looking back over my 35 years working as a veterinary surgeon in general practice, I consider myself a very fortunate individual. For around 25 years I worked in Sinclair and Wight's practice alongside my father Alf Wight (James Herriot) and his partner Donald Sinclair (Siegfried Farnon in the James Herriot books), two honest, decent and humorous men about whom I never had a bad word to say. Some excellent assistants have worked in the practice over the years, many of whom became real friends, and for the last 18 years of my professional life I practised with, among others, Peter Wright and Tim Yates, two of the longest-serving veterinary surgeons to have worked in Sinclair and Wight's practice in Thirsk. Together, we experienced the ups and downs, the triumphs and disasters that are the hallmark of the veterinary surgeon's life. There was never a moment of ill feeling between us, and it has been a privilege to work in such company.

It is with great pleasure that I write this foreword to Pete's book about his life as a vet, and his starring role in the highly successful Channel 5 TV series *The Yorkshire Vet*. The popularity of this programme has, in no small way, contributed to a marked increase in visitor numbers to the World of James Herriot Museum in Thirsk.

Jim with Peter and the statue of Jim's father, Alf Wight, at the World of Herriot Museum in Thirsk.

James Alfred Wight FRCVS OBE. 3rd Oct 1916 - 23rd Feb 1995
"James Herriot"

The introduction to each episode of *The Yorkshire Vet* displays the programme's links to James Herriot – "the world's most famous vet" – and this has greatly enhanced the popularity of the series. In return, the TV series has introduced a new generation of viewers to the name of James Herriot. Both *The Yorkshire Vet* and the Herriot name have benefited through their connection.

Peter gained some insight into the life of a vet while he was still at school. He spent some time with us at the practice in Thirsk, and from those early days we were impressed with his common-sense approach to the cases, his sensible questions and occasional suggestions, and above all, his enthusiasm for the job and his rapport with the clients. I remember my father saying to me, "I like this lad! Keep your eye on him; I wouldn't mind seeing him working here one day!"

One problem Peter had at that time was gaining admission to a veterinary school. Seriously high standards of A Level results were demanded and many, including some of his teachers at Thirsk School, were doubtful of his ability to attain the necessary marks. One of them, a close friend of mine, said to him, "two 'As' and one 'B'? I can't see it Pete! Have a go at it, but I just can't see it!" This must have acted as a spur to Pete, as, to his credit, he managed to gain the marks needed for admission to the Liverpool Veterinary School.

My father and I were delighted with his results, and took him to a Chinese restaurant in York as a celebration of his achievement. This was a step into the unknown for Pete, who had been brought up on straightforward wholesome Yorkshire country fare. I remember the look of horror on his face as he goggled at the alien heaps of noodles, bamboo shoots, and assorted meats and fish of many strange colours. He took a deep breath and began to eat; within minutes, all his doubts vanished. Pete had entered a whole new world; many are the fine oriental repasts that he and I have enjoyed together over the years.

There was always plenty of laughter in the practice when Pete was around. His dry Yorkshire humour is evident in the TV series, too, adding a refreshing twist to each episode.

I remember saying to him one morning, "There is a visit with a difference for you this morning, Pete. I want you to undertake an inspection at an ostrich farm".

"Oh yes?" he said, a ripple of surprise passing across his face.

"I think I should warn you: ostriches can sometimes be aggressive and, I am told, can reach a speed of 40 miles per hour from a standing start within a very few seconds."

Pete replied, a deadpan expression on his face, "I'll be doing 41!"

The Peter Wright that viewers see on *The Yorkshire Vet* is exactly the same man I remember from our veterinary days together. He comes across very naturally, as does the veterinary work performed on the TV screen. The veterinary surgeon's life has changed greatly since my retirement in 2001, but those abiding principles so dear to the profession – care, compassion, thoroughness – are still demonstrated by Peter and his colleagues. Like the real James Herriot before him, he is a credit to his profession; I know that many viewers of the TV programme will be fascinated to learn about the real Peter Wright.

Jim Wight
Author of *The Real James Herriot*

See chapter 2 for Peter's own thoughts about his A Levels.
See chapter 3 for Peter's account of his first Chinese takeaway.

Peter at work on another episode of *The Yorkshire Vet*.

A Life in a Day

It's 9am on Friday the 13th and I have a testicle in my hand. I'm not sure whether that counts as unlucky. If you're wondering, it belongs to a two-year-old Yorkshire terrier called Hugo. I've already found and removed the dog's other testicle, which was "retained", meaning it hadn't dropped when it should. The one in my hand is the second one, which I've separated him from while I'm at it; many owners want their pets castrated so they don't have to worry about pregnancies. It also calms some animals down.

The Yorkshire Vet TV crew is filming the whole procedure. Today director and cameraman David Terry and assistant producer Melissa Bartlett are on duty. Both of them are like coiled springs, waiting to jump into action. The TV crew is permanently camped out at Skeldale, our veterinary practice, on the lookout for stories to tell – wherever I am and whatever I do. They film at the surgery or jump in the car and join me when I go out on a call.

Today is bound to be like all other days I've had in my working life: something of a rollercoaster. Before beginning little Hugo's operation, I'd checked my emails and appointments and chatted to staff about some of the other bookings – including Kimmy, an 18-year-old Jack Russell with cataracts, who at that moment was crouching in the waiting room, shaking from head to toe with anger, not fear. She hates vets and won't tolerate anyone touching her, so had a muzzle on – it didn't matter that she was only in to have her claws clipped. My team didn't need to be told to be careful with their fingers, or to be gentle with her: that's a given with all creatures that come through our doors, great and small.

As I'd walked through the surgery, I'd checked on the other animals waiting for attention, stopping for a brief "chat" with Marnie, a boxer dog in to have a mass removed from his abdomen. I've had two of these fantastic animals myself. Marnie looked at me with a friendly if somewhat quizzical expression through the bars of his kennel; he was panting evenly, seemingly unperturbed by what lay ahead.

Inside the operating theatre, I'd given the already scrupulously clean table a final wipe, then put on a blue operating top and some surgical gloves. The sterilised surgical instruments, fantastically cleaned by an all-singing, all-dancing machine, were laid out nearby along with several types of thread for the stitches. All that remained was for Hugo to put in an appearance and prepare to part company with his testicles.

"How are you, my old friend?" I'd said softly to the dog.

David was filming as Melissa held aloft a huge fluffy microphone but, as usual, they were so discreet I could almost forget they were there. I injected Hugo with anaesthetic while Rachel, our head nurse, held him gently but firmly. He was quickly unconscious, his now unseeing eyes still slightly open. We laid him on his back, his tiny paws motionless in the air, so his genital area with its one visible testicle could be shaved. A surgical vacuum sucked away any remaining unattached hair. I've done thousands of castrations since qualifying as a vet in 1981, including many like this where one of the testicles hasn't descended. Although the operation hasn't really changed, anaesthetics are gentler now and recovery times faster. The only thing that seems to have changed is the filming.

Since *The Yorkshire Vet* began in 2015, I've had to get used to talking about my work for the camera, sometimes while I'm in the middle of a complicated operation. I think I've more or less got the hang of it, although I'm occasionally prompted to say more by a question from one of the crew. Today David asked how Hugo's testicles compare in size to those of a Great Dane. A Yorkshire terrier's testicles are obviously smaller, but I felt compelled to defend the little dog's manhood, so I said, "They're still reasonably sized."

As Rachel cleaned the area I was poised to cut into with a scalpel – I'd already had a feel and found the missing testicle – I briefly explained that dogs' testicles usually descend from the abdomen into the scrotum in the first few months of life. Sometimes, though, they either don't drop at all, or only partially. They might remain in the abdomen, making them tricky to locate and remove, or can be found nestling under muscle in the groin, which is easier to sort out. Removing these testicles is important: it can reduce the likelihood of future health problems, such as cancer.

Today the operation was relatively straightforward; Hugo's undescended testicle was quickly removed. Meanwhile, Monty, a spaniel on the operating table opposite, had an eyelid wart removed by young vet Guy Killick – who, like me, studied at Liverpool University. The muted sound of barking and traffic outside the operating theatre had no impact on our concentration.

I moved on to the second testicle, the descended one, and now here I am with it in my hand.

"He's better off without them," I say, holding up both of Hugo's testicles so the camera can see the difference in size between them. The retained testicle is much smaller. "Hugo wasn't a sex maniac, like some Yorkshire terriers," I add, in my element now. "They can be hypersexed and even vigorously go for cushions – a bit of an embarrassment when visitors turn up. Hugo is more of a 'pipe and slippers man', so if both testicles had descended, we could probably have left them. He won't miss them, and the worry of cancer is gone."

I stitch the little dog up and can't help pointing out that as we get older, we need our testicles less and less anyway. We all laugh.

By 10.15am David and I are in my car, its boot full of veterinary equipment and medicines as always. Melissa follows us in another vehicle holding the filming paraphernalia. We're soon driving slowly along a foggy country road heading to a 280-hectare (700-acre) farm where I've been many times before. Farmer Terry Bell and his son Richard have around 400 sheep, 500 beef cows and 160 hectares (400 acres) of arable land. They've lived here all their lives. My former boss Alf Wight – known to millions worldwide as author James Herriot – often visited. So too did my other boss, Donald Sinclair – Siegfried Farnon in the Herriot books – taking the same route I'm on today. Alf knew Terry's father Austin well, and sometimes took American tourists to the farm to watch and learn.

Alf and Donald both passed away in 1995, but their veterinary practice and the cycle of life continue; yet another lambing season is well underway. Richard has discovered that a ewe that gave birth two days ago has a prolapsed uterus. Because the ligaments have weakened and can't retain the womb, it's been pushed out. Although many sheep don't need human intervention during labour, some do; often farmers can help, but sometimes a vet is vital.

As we drive along, David and I have a quick chat, both intrigued by *The Yorkshire Vet*'s appearance on the popular Channel 4 reality show *Gogglebox*. We also briefly touch on the progress being made on David's bathroom renovations. Then he balances his camera on his shoulder and begins filming while I drive and explain where I'm going and why.

When we pull up in the farmyard I quickly don wellies and a dark green waterproof top and trousers; a massive German Shepherd sniffs around without menace before sloping away. I look far from fetching, but I'm here to work. I might have to look a little better later, though. There's a photoshoot for *The Yorkshire Vet* scheduled after lunch and I'll have to change into a nice shirt and tie, but right now my mind is on the poorly ewe.

I throw what I need in my vet's bag and locate Richard in a tractor shed. David and Melissa, who are filming my every move, sometimes trotting to keep up, follow me. We all stride swiftly through some deep mud and muck into a barn, where we see several sheep and cows and their wonderfully noisy babies. Richard expertly grabs hold of the ewe in question. She tries to run away while one of her two lambs looks on, anxiously bleating. I do a quick examination. The uterus is out – that's obvious – but there also seems to be far too much bright pink flesh on show. I realise that the ewe has been straining so much she's pushed out her anus. While she's not in any imminent danger, Richard and I both know that left to her own devices she could carry on pushing and eventually squeeze her intestines out. That would almost certainly result in her having to be put down, leaving two tiny orphans.

The atmosphere is focused but calm as Richard grabs a pile of hay to prop her up so her bottom is raised. I wash the affected area and give her an anaesthetic to dull the pain. I begin to push her body parts back inside to anchor them in place, my hand disappearing for a while. Gentle but consistent and controlled pressure does the trick, something I often watched Alf do when he was about the age I am now, and I was just a fresh-faced student.

When a stream of squelching sounds start coming from the ewe's nether regions, Richard jokes about the cameraman being the culprit.

"I did have a lot of fibre for breakfast," David quips.

The sheep bleats as if she thinks it's funny too.

I give my patient a shot of penicillin, then do the necessary stitching with a big needle and some thick material made from sheep intestine. The twin lambs are now nibbling hay a few metres away. Another lamb has very quietly just been born in the corner and is lying in the straw; a few cows peer on from nearby pens as the ewe gets ready to give birth again. The stitching finished, "my" sheep immediately scrambles to her feet and jogs off, turning back at one point to "baa" rather pointedly at me. Then her little ones pounce on her teats and begin suckling. Don't you just love spring?

Next stop is High Paradise, Judith Skilbeck's 10-hectare (25-acre) farm on the moors, right on the Cleveland Way, a popular route for ramblers. It really is a piece of paradise, nicely tucked away with a cafe, accommodation and camping spots; it even does the occasional wedding. A former police officer, now a rural crime coordinator, Judith has lived here for about 30 years and was featured on *The Yorkshire Vet* when one of her horses developed colic. She's up in the early hours every morning to check on her animals before going to work, and she has more to do when she gets home. She used to milk goats by hand, but doesn't have the time these days.

Today I'm checking on a cow called Foxglove. A few weeks ago I saw her shortly after she'd given birth, and although the calf — Eddie the Eagle, born during the Winter Olympics — was perfect and healthy, Foxglove developed a life-threatening pneumonia, unusual in an adult cow. The following day, when I went back to treat her, a massive snowdrift stopped me in my tracks despite my 4x4 — which, of course, Alf and Donald never had; they always carried shovels to dig themselves out if the weather turned nasty. I ended up walking the final stretch in a blizzard and met Judith's husband (even his beard covered in snowflakes) coming the other way to receive the necessary medication.

Today, the weather's cold and foggy, but at least there's no snow. David and Melissa are keen to film the final part of Foxglove's story; hopefully there'll be a happy ending. Camera in one hand, David opens the gate with the other. I sit snug as a bug in a rug in my warm car, thinking that with him along, I don't have to get out and open it myself. I'm also wondering when I might get a cup of tea. It's midday and I'm parched. It's yet another example of how times have changed: Alf and Donald seemed to be forever having cups of tea, slices of cake and fry-ups on their call-outs — or did it just seem like that? Nowadays, there hardly ever seems to be the time.

When we finally pull up at Judith's, I can hear lots of birds tweeting, but can't see them or the trees they're sitting in because of the fog. While Melissa dashes off to find Judith or her daughter Ginni I nod and smile at a couple of dogs barking furiously inside their locked compound. The nod seems to make them even more furious. I don't have a way with all animals.

Judith is soon leading us into a barn, which I'm always thrilled to enter. It's like stepping back in time, into a scene that Alf and

Donald would have recognised. Her place is just like the small-holdings of old – not the large-scale farming operations you usually see today. I'm reminded of scenes from my own childhood, and of another famous author, Enid Blyton, who wrote many farm stories for youngsters. The barn's full of cows, sheep, goats and ducks, and an assortment of their offspring; the happy sound they're all making is only a few levels below deafening. Five lanky lambs bounce up confidently and sniff me, letting me stroke them before head-butting my hands and legs. They're all bottle-fed as they don't have mothers; one, called Scotty the Bruce, was taken in by Judith when his mum was lost in the snow on another farm. Apparently, all the animals go to sleep when the lights are turned out in the evening. It's hard to believe right now, with this racket going on.

As a colourful cockerel struts around and a male goat unsuc-cessfully tries it on with a bored-looking female, Judith and I climb over a gate into Foxglove's pen. She's fine, and almost as if to prove it, she defecates – copiously – while I talk into the camera.

"She's not showing much gratitude, but it's lovely to see her looking so well," I say, ready as ever to inject a little humour. That's also something I got used to during Alf and Donald's time in the original practice at 23 Kirkgate, in the middle of Thirsk. Telling and listening to funny stories became part of the job; but I also talk about farmers like Judith being very attached to their animals. "Today is not just for Foxglove – it's for Judith, too."

Farmers don't have a nine-to-five life, I say, but their reward is seeing their animals happy, healthy and thriving. As Judith says, her lifestyle is uplifting, but when something goes wrong, "it turns my stomach inside out."

Next up is lunch. Today we're lucky because the farm's cafe, run by Ginni, is just a few metres away; but before we can order our Wensleydale cheese sandwiches and cups of Yorkshire tea, Ginni wants me to have a look at Stonker, one of her three Corgi cross dogs. She thinks he has something stuck in his throat. Luckily, there's nothing in there – I think tonsillitis is the problem.

Stonker and his brother, Sausage, once gobbled a huge pile of raisins, so I had to make them vomit – too many can give a dog kidney failure. Both dogs recovered, with Stonker even featuring in some of the publicity shots for *The Yorkshire Vet*. The dogs regularly appear on Ginni's Instagram account and people pop into the cafe specially to see them. They're far more popular than me or Julian Norton, the other Yorkshire Vet.

We finally devour a delicious lunch while Judith regales us with a sad tale about animals on the Moors occasionally falling down abandoned mineshafts left over from a time when people dug for jet, a black gemstone favoured by Queen Victoria. She then tells us an even sadder story about a man who murdered his wife and threw her body down one of the holes. He was caught after getting drunk in a pub and revealing what he'd done. A murderer – and a silly bugger.

We reluctantly drag ourselves away from the table, as we're now running late for the photoshoot with cameraman and photographer Paul Gay. I pop out to the car to collect a clean green shirt, chosen and beautifully ironed by my wife Lin. She always wants me to look my best, but it's not easy – I'm often covered in vomit, faeces and mucus.

Paul's first few shots in the barn at Judith's farm are constantly interrupted by the five head-butting lambs, which score high on the inquisitive scale. My attempts at making "baa" noises don't put them off (although the goats stare at me even more) so Judith distracts them with food. It's nice to see them all guzzling their powdered milk formula from five big bottles. They drink near a heat lamp too, a lovely touch given the chill in the air. Feeding time gives Paul the chance to position me among the haystacks and he captures me – warts and all – for eternity. He's a professional and it doesn't take long. Afterwards, I hear him quizzing Judith about chickens and chicken coops for his garden, which gives me a little thrill of pleasure. There's nothing better than people taking an interest in animals.

Around 2pm we say our goodbyes and do a few more driving shots before I unclip my microphone and return to Skeldale for afternoon surgery. The more vets there are in the practice, the quicker the clients and their pets are seen. David and Melissa have decided to stay out to film some footage of the countryside for *The Yorkshire Vet* and the camera watches me as I drive into the distance. At last the fog is clearing and I make good time, which is just as well, because the waiting room is already full when I get back. I'm quickly up to my ears in small animals. I think, as I always do, how lucky I am to have such a variety of work, with both pets and farm animals a regular feature of my working day. Two nurses cut matted fur from around a large rabbit's bottom while I check on Hugo the Yorkshire terrier. He's wide awake and none the worse for having no testicles.

Now it's Kierra's turn. She's an elderly collie dog with a hacking cough that doesn't want to go away. I check her mouth and listen to her heart and lungs. I also take her temperature, which she doesn't like, so she sits down on the thermometer. Knowing Kierra as I do – I've seen her many times – I diagnose tracheitis, an inflammation of her windpipe. She yelps when I give her an injection to reduce the swelling, but I don't take it personally. I recommend antibiotics for 10 days and soft food for what must be a very sore throat.

My next patient is a 10-week-old black cocker spaniel called Fig. He's glossy and new and adorable, and he's seeing me for his second vaccination. While I work, I chat to his owner about the pros and cons of tail-docking, before meandering on to how dogs are often cross when other pets arrive in their home. Fig's mum has two other dogs, and tells me that one recently stayed out all night in a grump because of the new arrival. It reminds me of my first boxer dog, Bert, who was madly jealous when we got a boxer puppy called Alf.

I could chat all day, but stop myself as there are many more patients to see. I momentarily think of a lady called Joan Snelling. Now retired, she was the secretary at Skeldale and also worked for more than 35 years at the old Kirkgate practice, the inspiration for the surgery in the Herriot books. Joan has known me since I was a teenager when I arrived at Kirkgate on work experience more than four decades ago. She would often tell me off for chatting too much to clients when we were busy – something she continued to do even when I became her boss.

I call the next patient, and five people – two women and three children, the oldest about eight – walk in with a tabby cat. It's minor mayhem for a few seconds as everyone settles down.

Amelia, about 14, is crouched in a pet carrier. Her owner says she seems a "bit funny in her mind".

"I see that a lot now," I reply. "Cats are living longer. In my early days it would have been unusual for a cat to get to this age, but now it's common."

I examine Amelia, who allows me to take her out of her box

without a fuss. She has beautiful gums and teeth and a strong heart, and although her hips are a little stiff she seems well. It's always hard to diagnose the early stages of dementia, but possible signs in a cat include being less adventurous and behaving strangely – maybe forgetting there's food in the bowl, or staring at the wall.

As Amelia jumps down onto the floor, her owner says she visited a vet in Harrogate last year who talked about arthritis.

"I can give Amelia injections for that later on if necessary," I say. "But I don't think she needs them now. Some arthritis medication can upset the kidneys."

Before I usher everyone out, the oldest child tells me she wants to be a vet when she grows up. Since *The Yorkshire Vet* began I hear this more than ever. I tell her to work hard at school.

When the last patient's been seen, I finally have time for a cup of tea and sit down to do some administration, tapping away on the computer keyboard, grateful I no longer have to write everything down on little cards. (No one could read my writing anyway.) As I'm working away, another young vet, Helen Blackburn, pops in to tell me a post-mortem is being done on a guinea pig, and that a bull has had treatment for a shattered shoulder. I think of the pain and wince on its behalf.

I then see receptionist and budgie fan Sylvia Binks put her arm around a colleague who's having a difficult few minutes in a workplace that's full of life, but sometimes death as well. I'm tired, but have an unmistakable feeling of satisfaction as I leave for home. I can't relax, though; I'm on call this weekend. I can't help but think of Alf and Donald and all the animals they treated, and I wonder what tomorrow will bring.

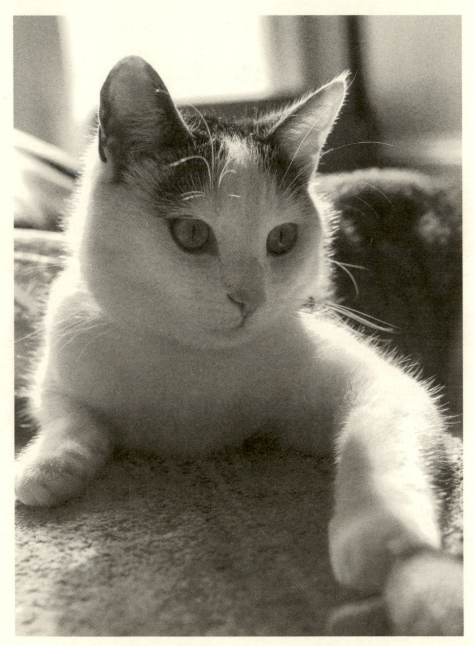

Toddy, the little rescue cat, who was found in a skip.

CHAPTER 1

Peter's Pets

I live not much more than a stone's throw from the damp, dark, cold cottage I was born in, not far from where the Kilburn White Horse is cut into the North Yorkshire hillside. Sometimes I stand at the window in our modern kitchen and gaze across the lush green fields towards Thirkleby, pointing out my very first home to visiting friends. I might be a Yorkshireman in my 60s but I'm not embarrassed to admit that when I'm alone, I even talk about the view to our one-year-old cat, Toddy, who's often slinking around nearby. He's a fast-moving ball of energy and mischief – in turn delightful, irritating and even scary to watch; he was hit by a slow-moving delivery van recently and had some painful cuts to show for it. I much prefer to see him sleeping serenely on my wife Lin's chest with his paw on her face than climbing erratically up the curtains and over the work surfaces, but given his history, I'm just glad he's alive and has a home – our home.

Toddy arrived at just the right time, not long after the deaths of our boxer dog Alf and RSPCA rescue cat Mary. They died within three weeks of each other, the latest in a long line of beloved pets. Soon afterwards, a tiny kitten – a veritable bundle of fluff about four weeks old – appeared at the surgery. He'd been found mewing, hungry and helpless, in a nearby skip. This charming little fellow pawed at me through the cage bars and as I lifted him out, he snuggled up as if he belonged. For Lin, it was love at first sight. Last Christmas Toddy played around our tree and sometimes inside it, his big eyes peering out from the middle, baubles and tinsel everywhere. I lost count of how many times I had to reassemble the decorations and branches, but the minor hassle was worth it: the house was transformed into a home again.

I like to think that as Toddy grows, he understands me at least a bit when I ponder the meaning of life during one of my increasingly regular trips down memory lane. I can't help but travel this road as I grow older; and the childhood cottage I can just about make out from my kitchen window, nestling in a village of about 20 houses, is one of the most poignant reminders of the rural domain of my first 13 years.

It was October 1956 when I greedily sucked in air for the first time in our two-bedroom house. My newborn cries came three months after the government had passed the Clean Air Act in response to a London smog that killed thousands. Then, a couple of weeks after I'd appeared, the young Elizabeth II visited Cumbria to switch on Britain's first nuclear power station. So my birth was squeezed between these two big events; but born more than 200 miles from Britain's decision-makers in Westminster, my infant self might as well have been in another universe – and what an idyllic one it was.

Our cottage was in the grounds of Manor Farm, not far from the market town of Thirsk. Farmed by Norman and Joan Knowles, it had arable land as well as many wonderful creatures: cattle, sheep, pigs, turkeys and chickens. I count myself lucky to have grown up on 70 hectares (180 acres) with none of the digital distractions of the 21st century and not much television either, this being the 1950s and 60s. I watched the children's programme *Blue Peter*, first on a black-and-white TV (my family had the first one in the village, watched by all the locals on the Queen's coronation day), but to my mind, my friends and I made more interesting things than the presenters. Our luxuries were the television set, a van, then a car, and annual holidays to Scarborough. Later we would go further afield, to Scotland. It was not an affluent childhood – unsurprisingly, given that both my parents left school at the age of 14 – but I could not have wished for a better environment to grow up in. We didn't have much, but we wanted for nothing. I was a shy child, perhaps hard to believe now. As a youngster it certainly helped that everyone knew me and I knew them. We didn't lock our doors and it was a big occasion if anyone moved in or out of the village.

My mother Jean was shy but fiery, a strict, no-nonsense mother and housewife who couldn't abide rudeness. She often felt children should be seen and not heard. The life you have as a child moulds you into the person you become, and she brought me up with a strong sense of right and wrong. She also did everything her role entailed at that particular place and time: all the cleaning, all the cooking, all the washing, and all without modern appliances to ease what must have been a heavy burden. I can see her in our kitchen now: chopping, peeling, stirring and kneading, forever hard at work feeding her family and turning a dingy room into a place of love and exacting manners. Food was, thankfully, plentiful, and the most important fruits of her labours were turned into tantalising smells and delicious meals that were quickly wolfed down by the three men in her life: my father Ken, my younger brother David and me.

We didn't use the front door of the cottage, entering at the back to avoid "paddling" in and making a mess in the front (best) sitting room, which we only really used at Christmas and when visitors called – although sometimes I'd lay out my farm set in there, using kindling sticks to make little fences. Mostly, though, I grew up in the kitchen. Like many homes back then, the cottage had an outside toilet. Winters can be cold in Yorkshire, so a trip to the loo often required a quick dash from our back door before pelting back inside. We had a washhouse, used on Mondays, with a "copper" (a big pot) in the corner to do the laundry in; there was a coalhouse and a log store, and another small outbuilding that we used for chopping wood and for storage. We'd often have bacon in there, hung high on ceiling hooks out of reach of the rats.

My father Ken, an easy-going and chatty man, was a labourer on Manor Farm. When he was small he lived with his parents in a cottage – since demolished – on the piece of land I now live on. Like me, he didn't move far. I was born in the semi-detached home that came with his job. His parents, my Granny and Grandad Wright, (Annie and Fred), lived in the other half of the cottage, and their home was our home too. Fred was the farm manager, a decent man respected by his workers. I remember him telling off vet Donald Sinclair, who'd later be my boss, for rushing around when he turned up at the farm one day.

"If you don't 'ave time to come, don't come," Grandad told him bluntly.

Donald apologised and calmed down, albeit temporarily. When I began working with him a decade or so later and got to know this charming and charismatic man, I realised he was always in a hurry.

When Grandad Wright wasn't telling off vets or managing the farm, he was raising his own chickens and selling them, plucked and oven-ready, to local butchers. My father would later take on this little business; as a child I watched, absorbed, as he dealt skilfully with chickens and turkeys, as well as a range of other creatures. Now, as a vet for more than 35 years, I have seen countless people rearing and looking after farm animals, but that doesn't always mean they are good at it. Not everyone can recognise when their creatures are ill or even what food to give them. My father and Grandad Wright, however, were both excellent stockmen. They learnt from experience, not books, and were frequently called upon by other locals to deal with their animals. This included slaughtering them, especially pigs. A lot of villagers in those first few years after the second world war kept a pig, and it was said they would make use of every little bit of it – except the grunt, as the joke would go. Waste was a dirty word.

Back in the home, Granny Annie, like my mother, had a similar waste-not-want-not approach to life. She was an incredibly hard-working housewife who also spent a lot of time meticulously cleaning and preparing hen houses, worrying about money and making her own rugs from rags. And if there was sometimes tension in the air with her daughter-in-law living next door, she didn't show it. Or maybe I was oblivious, as I spent most of my time roaming around outside. My brother and I thrived on fresh air and large helpings of good food and had no fewer than six doting adults around us (my mother's parents, Fred and Ena Duncalf, lived in a neighbouring village less than a mile away). We'd often stroll or, more usually, run over to see them, taking a route along the side of the beck, then over a footbridge. In bad weather we might be cut off from the Duncalfs when the water rose too high. There was a silver lining to that cloud, though: it also meant we couldn't get to the school bus, which drew up near their house. We would pray for heavy rain so we could have a day or two away from lessons. We wanted to be at home because the farm, the cottages and the village were not just home; they were a secure and generous slice of heaven.

There were a lot of distractions, like the tractors we would ride and fiddle with. I'd learnt to drive one by the time I was 12 and often used this skill to help out on the farm, including at harvesting and potato-picking time. With all the animals, farm workers and villagers to observe and talk to, plus a few toys and a handful of village friends to keep me interested, sociable and active, it's easy to see why I was more than satisfied with my lot. I never knew the meaning of the word "bored". With no through road and hardly any cars around, there was little worry about being knocked down; so I crawled, toddled, walked and ran in fields, farmyards and orchards. I had all manner of escapades and adventures, often likening myself and my mates to characters in Enid Blyton's *Famous Five* books. We were smugglers, goodies and baddies, unwittingly sharing our hay-bale dens with rats and mice in long roomy tunnels we built ourselves. When it snowed heavily, we'd sledge down the hill towards the beck, regularly ending up in it, wet and freezing but crying with laughter. My imagination and body ran riot, but I felt safe knowing I nestled in the bosom of my family.

The adults mostly got on with their busy lives, concentrating on making a living and being part of a close-knit community. My parents weren't hovering around their children all the time, like so many are now. They didn't have the time or the inclination, never even visiting my primary school, where they'd both studied too. Back then it just wasn't the done thing; they wouldn't have known what to say or what questions to ask. A friend who went to Cambridge University told me his parents hadn't met his teachers either. In so many ways, it was a different world in the 1950s and 60s. It can't have been easy for the grown-ups I knew, and I recall my mother being horrified when I mentioned that I might become a farm worker; she clearly thought life on a farm was too tough, with long hours and little pay. As children, though, we were protected from such sentiments, left to our own happy devices most of the time, although we had a few chores to do; I sometimes took the weekly bus to Thirsk with my mother to buy groceries. But mostly I played and played, then played some more. I was completely content, with few expectations of what I could or should be doing. To me, life was full of natural wonders. It may have rained a lot, but I also seem to recall being regularly cloaked in a warm and soothing light that showed the emerald countryside in all its glory.

Of course, as a child I never fully appreciated the full splendour of nature. I suppose I took it for granted. I wouldn't go out catching butterflies and putting them in jam jars nowadays, nor would I take eggs from birds' nests. And I certainly wouldn't recommend either of these practices to youngsters today, given the horrifying decline in so much of our wildlife in Yorkshire and beyond. But as a boy, when fields were smaller and hedgerows more plentiful, my friends and I would gather an egg from each species we found. We would blow out the insides and add the shells to our collections, getting as wide a variety as possible. We'd also dam the beck for fun or poach trout there; it was stocked and fished by a Leeds angling group. When I took some fish home for supper my mother really didn't like it (she was pretty squeamish about blood and guts for someone living on a farm), but my father appreciated it, while the farmer, Norman Knowles, knew what we were up to but turned a benevolent blind eye. We'd also go ferreting and catch rabbits, selling them to the butcher or eating them ourselves, although my mother didn't like that either. And she would never eat poultry, her excuse being that she'd been brought up with chickens and had seen the guts pulled out of them too many times. Beef was fine, as long as she didn't have to see the animal being killed. Early on, I accepted that the meat we ate came from dead animals and I tucked in with gusto, although I also enjoyed spending time with living ones.

There was a constant supply of fascinating and entertaining creatures to learn from in our village. I've now seen thousands of creatures being born, the first when I was just a wide-eyed child. I still get a pure feeling of exhilaration when I watch an animal take its first breath or first shaky steps, particularly a lamb in spring. It really is life-affirming. Of course, my acquaintance with death also began as a small boy, with an early realisation that some animals are slaughtered for their meat. Grandad Wright once killed a rat that had scurried up his trouser leg by squeezing it through the cloth, and I remember shooting a pigeon with an airgun just for fun. Before it even hit the ground, dead, I was overcome with remorse. I still try to avoid thinking about it. But sometimes the kindest thing to do for a terminally ill creature is to end its suffering. I lost count of the number of farm cats that Donald, my other boss Alf Wight and his son Jim euthanased after the feeble things were run over or, having poor immunity because of too much in-breeding, developed nasty diseases, such as liver cancer and leukemia.

Every creature I knew and grew up with, from the massive bulls and cows to the various dogs, cats and hens, was special, and each had its own personality. They were a significant part of the fabric of my childhood and while I cherished each one, I have a special place in my heart for dear old Spot, our black-and-white rabbit. We let him roam around the farm, and he was well known around the village because he wouldn't stay at home; he used to hop off on his own to graze and forage, to look around or to visit the neighbours. Rabbits are intelligent, active, inquisitive animals, which easily endear themselves to humans; about 1.5 million are kept as pets in Britain. Spot was loved by virtually everyone, and villagers would keep an eye out for him. He would bounce away enthusiastically to get some exercise or make his social calls before coming home to his hutch in our garden, where he spent his nights.

Then, one fateful day, he didn't come home. I was about eight, and I can still see myself running around and searching everywhere, shouting his name and asking if anyone had seen him. I was already distraught when I discovered Spot's broken body in a nearby field, literally a hop, skip and a jump away from our house. One of the bullocks grazing there had trodden on him and our lovely rabbit had been squashed to death. I was fond of the bullocks, too; one of them in particular was quite friendly, and used to saunter over and eat from my hand. But I was horrified at the sight of Spot's little body and it took me some time to get over his premature demise. It taught me that things just happen, and sometimes there's nothing to be done. Very early on I understood that life and death are closely intertwined; any creature, including you and me, can be here one minute and gone the next.

I learnt another harsh lesson about life through my beloved hens. I was hugely attached to a group of 12 that I looked after for a while. I even named them. Henny Penny and Chicken Licken were my favourites, and I really think they used to talk to me. I still find it soothing, the way hens will chat with people; they are such sociable creatures. One day before school, I went to the hen house, as I usually did, to say hello and check for eggs. All was eerily quiet as I approached. Then I saw a bloody bunch of feathers, and another, and another. Every hen was dead, cruelly killed by a fox. One poor bird had tried to escape and had got her neck caught in the gap between the gatepost and gate. She'd accidentally hung herself. I ran home, bawling. I never looked after hens again.

As well as an engaging variety of animal characters, I also grew up surrounded by some eccentric Yorkshire folk, their typical traits and attitudes brilliantly described in the Herriot books. Our cottage at Manor Farm was close to another farm run by the Medd family. They were well off, apparently owning steam engines, a threshing machine and even a street of houses in Bridlington. My uncle Richard (a bachelor and Granny Wright's brother) worked for the Medds, as did an elderly bachelor called George Barker. He had bought the village's oldest house in the 1920s and used to gather fruit from his orchard – glorious plums and apples – to take on the bus to Thirsk to sell at the market. I tend to think there's more to most people than meets the eye, and Mr Barker was no exception.

My father was an excellent handyman who could turn his hand to almost anything. One day Mr Barker had a problem with his electricity, so Dad popped round to see if he could help. I tagged along, always keen to see what was going on in the village, but when we arrived at Mr Barker's place, he looked at me sternly (he didn't smile much) and said, "I don't want that mischievous young man in 'ere!"

Dejected, I ran straight home. He must have felt guilty, because later he sent over two shillings for me. His frugal ways – frugal even by Yorkshire standards – were to rear up again, though, and would ultimately be immortalised in a Herriot book.

If the Wright family hens were not laying enough (and after my 12 were killed, that happened more often), we bought eggs from Mr Barker. My mother would send me to him to stock up, often on a Saturday, so there'd be enough for all the baking, including Sunday's delicious Yorkshire puddings. One day I arrived home with what I thought were a dozen eggs, but when Mam counted them out in the kitchen she found just 11.

"He must have miscounted. Tell 'im next time," she said.

The following week I was apprehensive when I went to get our eggs.

"We were an egg short last week, Mr Barker!" I managed to stutter.

His eyes narrowed as he stared down at me, then he paused for just a beat before saying: "You're right, young man! There was 11, I remember now – but one of 'em was a double-yolked 'un!"

A double-yolked egg occurs when the ovary releases the next yolk too early, and the shell forms around both yolks; it's fairly common, and some hens only lay double yolkers.

Years later, Alf Wight chortled away when I told him this tale. Little did I know that a version would appear in his book *The Lord God Made Them All*, published in 1981. The scene involved the young vet James Herriot buying a dozen eggs from a farmer called Mr Bogg, who was "tightfisted, a byword in a community where thrift was the norm". Told later there had only been 11 eggs, Mr Bogg gave the same response as Mr Barker; Alf captured the exact same language beautifully. He also used the egg story in after-dinner talks, and his son Jim still does; his heartwarming speech at a 2016 event marking the centenary of Alf's birth included the yarn. I was there with more than 300 other people including the main actors from the BBC TV series, *All Creatures Great and Small,* who were reunited for the first time in many years. I enjoyed hearing the laughter that evening at one of my treasured childhood memories.

To be fair to Mr Barker, who can't defend himself – he's long gone – he might not have been as tightfisted as he seemed. It was possible he knew the egg contained two yolks, because such eggs are usually much larger than regular ones. I can't recall my mother or me cracking the egg to find out definitively, but anyway, I've learnt that it's generally good to probe gently for a person's backstory and give them the benefit of the doubt.

It's said that when Mr Barker died in 1976 he left tens of thousands of pounds – a tidy sum, and obviously worth a lot more in today's money. Some went to a local farming family and some, I heard, to Barnardo's, the charity founded in Victorian times to care for vulnerable young people. I would love to know what Mr Barker's inspiration was and what his own childhood was like. Life was difficult for many people in the early years of the 20th century, especially those not born into affluent households and before the days of the welfare state. As Jim Wight says: "The money made by farmers, they earned with blood."

It seems Mr Barker was fundamentally a decent man, even if he was unable to restrain himself from counting one egg as two. His lifetime approach to money is perhaps best summed up by an event at his funeral. My father was one of the pallbearers, and as they shuffled along with the dead man perched on their shoulders, one man happened to mention that the bearing fee they'd all received had recently gone up.

"You shouldn't 'ave said that in front of George; 'e'd 'ave carried 'imself!" said my father.

All of them – and the body just above – shook with laughter.

Thinking of my father's broad Yorkshire tones, I can sympathise with the difficulties of outsiders trying to grapple with this variation of English. Even growing up in the region, it took me some time to get to know all its unusual words and phrases. When I first heard Granny Wright talk about "a nest of pissimers", someone had to explain that she meant a nest of ants. If it was a bit "parky", it was chilly, and if you heard a farm worker say, "It's a bad job," you knew something was amiss even if they weren't showing any emotion on their weatherbeaten faces.

"She's only a one-pap't 'un!" (she's only got one teat) was a fairly common phrase, and one I recall hearing years later from the best stockman I've ever known, Howard Bosomworth. I'd just helped one of his ewes give birth to three lambs in my early years as a qualified vet. Howard meant the mother couldn't feed all three babies as she only had one teat, but he almost immediately began to laugh, realising how pessimistic he sounded after witnessing the miracle of new life: indeed, three new lives.

Another Yorkshireism that transports me back to my childhood is "pikelet", meaning crumpet. Just hearing the word conjures up images of thick, savoury cakes oozing melted butter, and tables groaning under the weight of some of the best food I've had the privilege of gorging on. Roast lamb, pork or beef (goose on Christmas Day at the Duncalfs'), but always mint sauce and Yorkshire puddings to start with. The puddings were huge and fluffy and I've always said, no Yorkshire pudding is ever as good as the one made by your own mother. By eating them first, the idea was supposedly that "them that eats most puddings gets most meat". Of course, by the time the meat – the most expensive food – arrived, we were too full to eat much of it.

There was a never-ending supply of pies too, often apple or rhubarb, or whatever else was in season. I'd run into Granny Wright's pantry next door to find even more goodies: homemade scones, teacakes, buns and just-baked bread. What a sight – and what a smell. It mattered not a jot that we didn't have the money to visit the famous Betty's Tea Rooms in York and Harrogate; we had our own version of afternoon tea at home. Imagine coming home to all that after a long day playing in the fields, or building up an appetite kicking a football around for hours. Pure bliss. Except, of course, when I kicked my ball through the kitchen window one day and the beautiful spread was showered with glass. Mam smacked my bottom and sent me straight to bed.

We also had mountains of fresh vegetables from Grandad Duncalf's vegetable patch in his front garden; I've never tasted better new potatoes, which were usually topped off with lashings of butter. As a child I wasn't interested in growing food, but now I appreciate Grandad's skill. My lettuces and cabbages have often been the victim of slugs, rabbits and some truly mysterious killers, but still I persevere in the hope I can raise myself to Grandad's dizzying growing heights. I think of his green fingers whenever I pass his old house.

Sometimes I drive past my primary school in a nearby village. I wasn't there much at first as I managed to get one illness after another, including measles and tonsillitis. I even chopped off the end of a finger in the kitchen door when my brother slammed it shut. Luckily, the doctors sewed it back on. Mr Cluston, the school attendance officer, visited our home so often to see where I was (we didn't have a telephone then) that he and his wife became family friends. But while my dad had often played the fool at school, once putting the teachers' cups and saucers in a nearby stream and pelting them with stones, that wasn't to be my way once I did start making it to lessons regularly.

I have always been scared of failing, and at just five and six I hated getting an answer wrong in class – or, even worse, not being able to answer the question at all. I was shy and self-conscious and it embarrassed and upset me to not perform well. It felt like failure. I must have quickly realised that the only way to avoid this feeling, and occasionally the laughter of my classmates when I got something wrong, was to know the answers. I had quite a bit of school to catch up on, having missed so much with my various ailments, but I was determined, regularly chanting my times tables alone at home. My parents left me to it; they bought me books and donated items for the school's fundraising efforts, but that was it. Granny Duncalf and I read to each other, but there was no pressure at home to succeed; people from our walk of life were not expected to achieve academically. I was expected to go to school, and then get a job. But when I realised that I was not only getting a kick out of reading and finding things out, but giving more and more correct answers in class to my skilled and caring teachers, I felt good about myself. I enjoyed that feeling and wanted to keep feeling it.

I have always had a logical mind and could easily understand my times tables, but it wasn't so easy to work out why I was bullied. There's no other word to describe what a particular group of older lads put me through until they moved up to secondary school. Their actions served to make me even keener on lessons, as only in class or at home could I escape their taunting clutches. Thankfully there was no social media then, or they might have had access to me at all hours. My mother went to see the ringleader's mother, but it didn't help. In fact, it just deterred me from telling anyone else. Plus, the bully boys were sneaky and managed to play their nasty tricks when the teachers weren't looking. During some terrifying winter playtimes the bully boss and his cronies would make huge snowballs and crash them onto my head while I stood there, sobbing. Sometimes they'd pile on top of each other in a big heap with me at the bottom. I was already claustrophobic after a disastrous trip to the dentist; she'd tried to pull a tooth out and had pinned me down by the arms. Being jumped on made it worse. Sometimes when the bullies were on top of me I couldn't breathe properly and actually thought I might die, but my high-pitched screeches only encouraged them further. All this went on for over two years.

I managed to get a little revenge when I began doing well at sport, especially football. I was able to run rings around the ringleader, who sometimes joined in a kickabout with my friends and me after school. I also became head boy when the bullies went to secondary school, which boosted my confidence. Decades on, and not surprisingly, I was keen to promote anti-bullying schemes when I became a school governor.

For my 60th birthday in 2016 I took a flight in a glider, not far from home. I had to climb into a tiny cockpit while being filmed for *The Yorkshire Vet*. Strapped in by a seatbelt and wearing a parachute, I felt more trussed up than an oven-ready chicken, but I managed to control my panic and overcome my claustrophobia for the cameras. I was relieved to discover that once up in the air and looking down over such an inspiring and beautiful open space, I was fine; I even enjoyed it.

So eventually, I cast aside the memories of being bullied. Perhaps I should even thank the culprits: because of them I hurled myself into my schoolwork, which eventually led me to university and my career as a vet. And despite their best efforts, my primary school days were not all bad. In April 2017, I found myself posing for a photo surrounded by fabulous tractors, with a large smile on my face and an arm wrapped around a wonderful woman. I'd been invited to open an "Easter Eggstravaganza" in the village of Sessay, where I'd gone to school, and the lady in question was Heather Corner, who'd been my primary school teacher and headmistress. Now a great-grandmother in her 90s, Heather still plays an active role in the community she's been part of for more than six decades. As a *Yorkshire Vet* fan she'd asked me on behalf of the village hall committee to attend the Easter event, which included a driving display by 47 tractors. With Heather as my hostess, the day couldn't have gone better if I'd met the Queen herself.

Heather is the epitome of what I consider to be a strong Yorkshire woman: wise, hardworking and dedicated, rolling up her sleeves and getting on with life despite some tough challenges. She grew up on a farm of about 30 hectares (70 acres), her mother a headteacher and her father a tenant farmer. His eyesight was poor and Heather had to help him, especially with the animals – bringing lambs into the world and milking cows by hand before and after school. She loved it and actually wanted to be a vet; the family's vet at the time even recommended it. But as her parents couldn't afford for her to study veterinary medicine, she became a teacher instead. A mother of three, she was widowed in her 40s but continued to work, making a mark on countless impressionable young minds with her warmth, knowledge and enthusiasm. Our school, a small Victorian building, had a separate canteen at the back, which we had to walk to in all weathers for lunch. There were no flush toilets and no heating, but none of that seemed to matter. There were school trips, Christmas parties, the Magna Carta's 750th anniversary celebrations and theatrical productions such as Shakespeare's comedy *The Taming of the Shrew*.

Heather also had a positive impact on our young bodies, insisting we do some sport or exercise every day. We played all sorts, including rounders and cricket, and took part in organised snowball fights (two teams, and we could only hit below the knee) and sports days on the village green. In good weather we'd go outside for lessons and often did some gardening. She'd tell us to "feel the wind, then write a poem" or "visit the beck to see the kingfishers". What an education. What an inspiration. All her pupils remain in her debt.

I received a letter from Heather after she'd enjoyed a particular episode of *The Yorkshire Vet*. I'd been filmed at the top of Sutton Bank; there's a beguiling view from the top of this steep hill on the edge of the moors. As I surveyed the scene I'd talked about how much the countryside meant to me. It moved my old teacher to write me a letter in which she quoted from a poem we'd studied at school: 'Leisure' by William Henry Davies.

> *What is this life if, full of care,*
> *We have no time to stand and stare? —*
> *No time to stand beneath the boughs,*
> *And stare as long as sheep or cows...*

Heather was pleased to see me finding time to stand and stare at Yorkshire's finery, just as she'd encouraged us to do as children.

Young people these days go on holidays overseas that I could never have imagined; but as a child, I couldn't get enough of Scarborough. I'm not the only one who has ever loved this Yorkshire seaside town, hugely popular when I was young and at a time when most people never thought of going abroad. I later found out that during the second world war, Alf Wight enjoyed being stationed in the town's Grand Hotel for a few months, although he slept on uncarpeted floors, and the windows were held open by nails.

To me, a small child who rarely left his immediate environment, the annual journey to Scarborough in July was almost as exciting as the final destination. Before we had a car, we'd go on the bus (a red one from Thirsk marketplace), with Granny and Grandad Duncalf coming along too. My next-door grandparents preferred to stay at home, and anyway, someone had to look after all the animals. It felt like we were travelling to the other side of the world, but this fun-filled paradise wasn't much more than 40 miles away. Still, it was (it still is) an unforgettable thrill to spot the sea for the first time.

I shared a room with my parents in a guest house (the same room, in the same place, with the same landlady every year) overlooking the seafront. I rode donkeys on the golden sands, splashed and swam in the sea, and ate mouth-watering fish and chips before taking on the one-armed bandits. Then there were spectacular knickerbocker glories to devour in the Harbour Bar ice-cream parlour. (Coincidentally, about 20 years later, one of my favourite jobs as a newly qualified vet was visiting a dairy herd at Ampleforth College, a private Catholic school not far from our practice, which supplied the Harbour Bar with its milk.) But most of all I enjoyed the magical offerings of Scarborough's Peasholm Park, including its little railway and boating lake. I still occasionally visit "Scarbados", as some of the locals like to call it; the panoramic views from the castle are sublime, and these days tourists can hurtle across the waves on a fantastic speedboat ride. Elton John, Tom Jones and other famous entertainers have even performed in the town. Last year, I returned with some old friends and we had a fabulous few hours wandering in the sunshine and sitting on the beach, finishing with ice creams from my old haunt.

That's not to say, however, that every nostalgic trip goes according to plan. I remember taking Lin and our two children for a day out in Scarborough in the early 1990s. I'd been working really hard and thought a family trip would be a nice little break.

I hadn't been to the town for around 20 years, as when I was an older child my parents had started taking my brother and me to Scotland instead. I preferred Scarborough: it rained less and there were no midges to drive us crazy.

Lin was tired out looking after the kids, a job she often did alone as I worked so much. She initially thought the Scarborough expedition would be too much hard work, but eventually agreed to indulge me. Our children, Emily and Andrew, were at an age when they'd ask, "Are we there yet?" every 30 seconds.

We set off in a light drizzle, and my early burbles of delight at the picturesque villages and alluring countryside along the way were met with regular howls of "I don't like it!" and "I don't want to!" from the back. There was also an ominous and disapproving silence at my side in the front.

If it started badly, it went downhill from there. Difficulty parking was followed by a rapidly dipping temperature and heavy rain, meaning no donkey rides. The guesthouse I'd stayed in as a child was run down, with paint peeling from the window frames. We rescued the situation for a while in Peasholm Park, but soon found our feet sticking to the carpet of my favourite fish and chip restaurant. Another nail in the coffin of the day (but not the final one) was the slimy, greasy food served by a grumpy waitress with a mucky apron.

By this point the children had two settings: moaning or crying, and Lin and I were no longer on speaking terms. The three of them hardly touched their meal and I had to force mine down, determined to get something from the day and not completely lose face on this nightmarish tour of my long-lost youth.

"How about we go on to Whitby?" I blurted out, on a whim.

It was on the 19-mile drive up the coast that I felt my stomach begin to churn. I needed a toilet and I needed one fast. I hit the accelerator and felt none of my usual interest in the enchanting seascape. When we reached Whitby I barely noticed the sun shining on the beautifully manicured lawns and flowerbeds; I merely saw a heaven-sent public toilet and was grateful I wasn't hallucinating. I screeched to a halt, jumped from the car and burst through the graffiti-covered doors, speeding past a solitary figure having a pee. Entering a cubicle, I slammed the door shut with seconds to spare.

It was while I was sitting on the toilet, relieved and thinking the day had finally taken a turn for the better, that I noticed something moving just ahead of me. Leaning forward, I saw a hole in the cubicle door where the lock should have been. There was an eye staring back at me. Then, in a flash, it was gone. I wasn't brave enough to confront the voyeur in the narrow confines of the toilet block, so I pulled up my trousers and ran out, glaring at a long-haired man in a trench coat standing in the corner.

At least something good emerged from our disastrous trip, though; the "pervert in the toilet" story finally brought a smile to Lin's face, and she enjoys retelling the tale to this day.

A teenage Peter with Rex, his parents' Labrador.

CHAPTER 2

Dave's Halitosis

I peered with fascination, but no fear, into Dave's gaping mouth. He was a delightful English bull terrier, all 25kg (4st) of him; his only apparent defect was his exceptionally bad breath. Under general anaesthetic I established he had an ulcerated gum and some rotten teeth. I removed them with various implements, including a drill (instead of Latin I did woodwork at school, a skill that often comes in handy during surgery) and finished off with a scale and polish.

Dave's human owner, Steve, was delighted that his pet had a healthy mouth again and no more halitosis.

"They're tough dogs – don't show pain," he said. "Whatever's happening, they still wag their tails, God love 'em!"

He and Dave were soon home, with the friendly animal tucking into his favourite food: rice pudding, sardines, chicken stew and tripe. A happy ending, which is one of the best things about my job.

Alf Wight would regularly say to his proteges: "Always do your best." I often remind myself of these wise words. Working as a vet doesn't always go the way we'd like, as nature can be cruel. Sometimes it can't be beaten, despite our best efforts and scientific progress. Sometimes nature *shouldn't* be beaten.

I often see a sparrowhawk in my garden, preying on small birds. Unpalatable as it might be for me to watch over breakfast, it's nature in action and the sparrowhawk needs to eat too. But at least I can try to rectify some of the things that go wrong with an animal's health, like Dave the bull terrier's bad breath. A minor victory, but a victory nonetheless.

I was Dave's dentist in 2015, in the first episode of the first series of *The Yorkshire Vet*. It reminded me of an incident when I was a self-conscious teenager. I'd been a big fish in a tiny pond at primary school before becoming a tiny minnow at secondary school in Thirsk. One day in 1974, a teacher asked me if I'd consider a career in dentistry. I disdainfully dismissed the idea, but John Ward's question in that school corridor set in motion a chain of events that altered the course of my life. I might never have had a veterinary career if not for that day, and I would probably never have worked with Alf Wight and Donald Sinclair. I might never have met my wife, as she worked near the vets' practice, or had my children. And I certainly wouldn't have been in *The Yorkshire Vet*.

Mr Ward was my chain-smoking A-level chemistry teacher and head of careers, a popular man usually covered in chalk dust. At Thirsk I had continued to enjoy and excel at maths, and had become increasingly interested in the three sciences. Later in the sixth form, Mr Ward would often tell me I needed to fully grasp the fundamentals of my subjects and push myself harder. Sometimes he'd say this over a pint in Thirsk's "Ye Olde Three Tuns" pub (locals always called it "The Little Three") on Finkle Street, where my dad and grandads drank on a Saturday night. Some of us were slightly under the legal drinking age, but Mr Ward's decision to drink with us, a concessionary nod to the young adults lurking inside our gangly and acne-ridden bodies, made us feel special. Most importantly we felt, and were, listened to; we used to open up to Mr Ward in this neutral environment. For youngsters like me, whose parents were loving but not really interested in schoolwork, homework or exams, these relaxed chats with an intelligent and resourceful teacher were invaluable. They allowed me to get a sense of some of the other possibilities in life. Years later, I was chuffed when Mr Ward came to my wedding; he'd even managed to clean off the chalk dust from his jacket for the event. When he died, I was not the only former student to feel his absence, and recall all those pearls of wisdom in The Little Three.

Back in that school corridor, and some time before I took my A Levels for the first time, Mr Ward's question about what I was considering for a career was brisk. I'd had a thought or two about engineering, but nothing coherent, so didn't mention it. At the time, I was far more focused on sport. Football, cricket, tennis and swimming – I loved them all, and was sports captain for my school house. Although I did my schoolwork reasonably diligently, I didn't focus much on homework, let alone have cohesive opinions on what to do when I left school.

"I don't know, sir," I said simply.

Mr Ward dived straight in. "How about becoming a dentist?"

I was not impressed. With the bravado of youth, I told him the thought of peering into other people's mouths all day filled me with horror.

"So what about veterinary science?" he shot back.

I think Mr Ward must have seen the cogs whirring in my brain and realised he was on to something. I didn't just brush off his suggestion. I was interested.

Luckily, Mr Ward knew how he could help; he had connections he could introduce me to. He'd taught Alf Wight's son Jim (13 years older than me) and had sometimes taken him and other pupils on youth hostelling trips. He knew the Wight family well, whereas I'd met Alf and Jim on only a handful of occasions. Alf had come to the farm to castrate some young bulls when I was about seven. He seemed a nice man who didn't get flustered, and was careful with the animals; I remember him wearing a big long waterproof coat and wellington boots. But I certainly didn't know any of the vets well. Manor Farm was just one of their many clients and I was only a child, a passive onlooker in a grown-up world.

The school corridor conversation came well before the height of Alf's Herriot fame and the TV series that gave an even bigger boost to his growing popularity. At this point, many of his books hadn't even been written. I had, though, read the first one, *If Only They Could Talk*, which was given to me by my uncle Brian, my mother's brother. He was a farmer and he handed it over, saying he'd found it entertaining. I enjoyed it and was impressed that the wit and ways of so many Yorkshire characters had been captured so well.

Mr Ward said he'd have a word with Jim, who'd qualified as a vet in 1966 and not long afterwards had come back to Thirsk to work with his father. The teacher said he would try to fix up half a day's work experience for me to see what I thought. Who would have guessed that one simple conversation in a school corridor would open the door to a new world? His flash of inspiration would, ultimately, lead to me pulling out rotten teeth from Dave the bull terrier's foul-smelling mouth with the TV cameras filming my every move. Perhaps Mr Ward thought I'd have made a better dentist than vet, but if so, he wasn't completely wrong in his assessment of me. I've lost track of all the mouths I've probed and the teeth I've pulled, from those of dogs and cats to hamsters, rabbits and horses.

Not long after my innocuous chat with Mr Ward, I was on my way to the Sinclair and Wight veterinary practice at 23 Kirkgate in Thirsk, known as Skeldale in the Herriot books. It's an imposing three-storey Georgian building, next door to the Royal British Legion and just down the road from the beautiful church where Alf married his beloved Joan (Helen Herriot is based on her). I had visited the practice a couple of times with my father. Once was when I was about 10: Jim helped us out with a farm cat with a dislocated hip, but we had little money to pay for treatment so Jim recommended leaving it to mend on its own in the hope that a "false joint" would form.

Years later, during my work experience and then later as a veterinary student, I found out more about this kind of treatment. I learnt that Jim was counting on nature securing the top of the cat's femur to its pelvis, allowing the little creature to continue moving. It worked, and also worked for our limited budget; although the injured leg was a little shorter than the other back leg, within a few weeks the cat was climbing trees again.

I don't remember thinking about the cat with the false joint as I embarked on my first day of work experience in Kirkgate. I was no doubt bewildered and nervous, being shy, and I expect I walked gingerly up the three steps to the solid red door, which led to an inner door with its glass top half and distinctive clicking latch. I'd love to say my approach and entrance are scorched onto my memory, but they're not. What I do remember is an overwhelming feeling of meeting my destiny head-on. From the first few moments, I would have gladly taken my sleeping bag and moved in. I was totally captivated and knew from that day forwards that I would become a vet, or at least try to become one.

The surgery buzzed with warmth and activity. There was lots of laughter and friendly banter and a wonderful generosity of spirit. The clunky old-fashioned telephone rang almost incessantly. I heard "Good morning, Sinclair and Wight?" time and time again; it was music to my ears. The telephone number was 2297. Later it would become 22297 and finally 522297, the number we still have in our practice today, despite moving in 1996 to Skeldale, our bigger premises on the outskirts of Thirsk (as seen in *The Yorkshire Vet*). Dogs at the Kirkgate surgery had initially been examined in the hallway on a small ledge that pulled out from the wall (the ledge is still there), only later in consulting rooms. There had been no need for a proper room for small animals in Alf and Donald's early days, because most of the veterinary work at that time was still being done on farms and smallholdings. There were far fewer pets than there are now and most of them hardly ever saw a vet.

I eagerly took in the atmosphere, as well as the smell of the medicines, the surgical spirit and the anaesthetic. I caught glimpses of Alf, Donald and Jim as they came in and out, doing jobs logged in the day book. In all the hustle and bustle, the vets never knew from one minute to the next what they would be doing. They couldn't guess what a telephone call might bring. It wasn't lost on me that the job involved a lot of work with farm animals outside, my favourite place. I also saw that I would need to use my brain. This is for me, I thought, feeling both overawed and lucky that I'd been welcomed into this magical place.

Over the next few weeks, months and years I became a regular visitor to 23 Kirkgate, and increasingly a helpful pair of hands as my knowledge and confidence grew. I gained invaluable practical work experience after school, during weekends and in the holidays while studying for my A Levels. I also returned to the surgery regularly during university breaks. The three vets were beginning what would be a decades-long process of showing me what they did, and teaching me their basic ethos of respecting clients and colleagues, not to mention the animals.

The vets naturally ruled the roost, but secretary Joan Snelling was the glue holding the team together. She started working at 23 Kirkgate as a 15-year-old in 1959, initially as a receptionist. I was a full partner when she retired 44 years later. From my first day on work experience, I watched Joan charm her way through some difficult calls, often with stressed and demanding farmers. I was still shy, so initially dreaded answering the phone; but Joan took it all in her stride. When she took a call she would write down the key details, knowing that the one or two sentences she recorded in the day book could only hint at the drama involved in, say, a difficult calving or the treatment of a poorly pig. Not long ago I popped into Kirkgate (now the award-winning World of James Herriot visitor attraction) and had an emotional flick through some of the old day books stacked in the dispensary. Marked next to each job was an initial, with A for Alf, D for Donald and J for Jim.

I didn't want to get in anyone's way during my work experience at Kirkgate, but as time went on and I became more of a known quantity, I was allowed out on more calls. I occasionally went with Alf and Donald, although they regularly sidled off and did farm visits without me. When I was qualified myself, I came to appreciate how nice it can be to go out on your own, especially to family farms, where you are often invited in for a drink and a chat with clients who also become friends. Anyway, I didn't expect the Kirkgate crew to want a blushing teenager tagging along.

I did go out a lot with Jim, though. He was the youngest of the three vets – the closest to me in age. Years later, he and his wife Gill would become godparents to my children. In the early days, Jim particularly appreciated my help with "rodeos", the word we often used to describe difficult cattle jobs that were more suited to younger and fitter men like us than to Alf and Donald. Alf was already in his mid-50s and Donald in his early 60s when I began my work experience.

The rodeos, hard work with some really feisty animals, included procedures like dehorning – removing horns from bull calves, which Alf taught me to do – castrations and testing for TB and brucellosis, which are notifiable diseases. That means the government must be informed when they are discovered in farm animals, as they can be passed on to humans. Alf and I both suffered from brucellosis during our careers, but more on that later.

To confirm a diagnosis in an animal, blood is often taken from its tail, which is no easy task, and certainly difficult for one vet to do alone. That's why Jim was so often glad of my help. Testing a herd of cows for tuberculosis (TB) is also considered a rodeo job, because it involves injections into the skin of an animal's neck after restraining it in a portable "crush", a special stall. I liked this kind of work. I always aimed to please and tried to make myself useful, including opening farm gates so the appreciative vet could stay in the warmth of the car. And, I admit, I got a kick out of playing the Yorkshire cowboy, particularly wrestling with bullocks. My years growing up on a farm stood me in good stead. I enjoyed being with stock and was comfortable around them. Alf and Donald usually chose the lighter jobs anyway, as at that point they no longer felt like castrating 30 wild bulls, even if they could. As time went on, Alf in particular loved what he called "nice little visits", by which he meant treating straightforward illnesses rather than having to grapple with unpredictable herds.

Later, when I was a veterinary student, Alf took me out on lambings, allowing me to have a feel inside the ewe. He told me not to rush and make sure there was plenty of lubrication; the farmer had usually already had his dry, rough, big-as-shovel hands inside the animal, making the job more difficult. I heard more than one farmer say, "It's not thou we need, Alf Wight. It's them little doll 'ands o' thine that's needed!"

Alf, whose small hands didn't really look strong enough to tackle a difficult birth, would nod politely before inserting an arm into the ewe's vagina. Sooner or later he would expertly ease a newborn lamb or two onto the straw. He was a master of patience and oozed calm. I always endeavoured to follow in his footsteps – even if I did lack his "doll 'ands".

At the surgery, sometimes one or more of the vets would be around and a few of us would have a cup of tea, a biscuit (sometimes a small, juicy apple from the garden) and a chat. I mostly listened in the early days, as I still lacked confidence. Joan sat in the office at the front, a large bright room with a big window overlooking the street. Her desk was in the corner on the left-hand side as you went through the door, next to a big bench with shelves full of files with paperwork piled on top. She worked facing the wall and was some distance away from the window and the second desk next to it, where one of the vets sometimes sat. Donald made her face the wall as he didn't want her to be disturbed by the farmers who came to Thirsk in their droves on market Mondays and would pop in to settle an account or, more likely, to be sociable after a pint or two. At one point, he even brought in a dressing screen from home to put around her desk, hoping it would hide her away from view. It failed to dissuade most farmers. They simply popped their heads around it and did their best to distract Joan with amiable, sometimes beer-laden comments.

In those early years of work experience, the kettle always seemed to be on. Donald and Alf would usually stand side by side, leaning against a storage heater with their mugs of tea. From there they had a good view of the window and all the characters, animal and human, coming in or going past. We'd nurse our drinks and laugh at the stories of what the vets called their "failures". Donald often said, "If there are mistakes to be made, I've made them."

We'd also discuss football, touching on Alf's joys, worries and fears about his beloved Sunderland, or amateur dramatics, thanks to Jim, who was in a local society. He was, and is, a good storyteller too, with a great sense of humour, and his own stories always seemed to involve the words "the worst case I have ever seen". Some farmers also latched on to his dramatic ways, and had some good-natured fun at his expense. I always enjoyed stopping off for a pint or two with Jim after a sweaty and exhausting day at work. It was not only a chance to have a drink and a bite to eat, but an opportunity to tune into another live and thrilling episode from the world of Sinclair and Wight that I was so desperate to be a full-time member of.

⅋

I remember Jim and I once visited Donald at home in Southwoods Hall, which was in a nearby village. Donald was married to a lovely lady called Audrey and he would often say to Jim, "Come and have a cup of tea with me and Auntie Audrey."

At the time, I had no idea what kind of place they lived in; it could have been a semi-detached bungalow for all I knew. The route took us through some woods and up a long, winding drive next to lush grass fields. When we came to a halt outside a picture-postcard hall nestling at the foot of the Hambleton Hills, I was mesmerised and under the impression, as I gazed at this magnificent building, that Donald must be making a very good living. It made me even keener, if that were possible, to join the profession.

Jim and I rang the bell before being greeted warmly by Donald and two bouncy Labradors. We followed them into a large and cosy drawing room that looked out on some of the finest views I've ever seen of the Vale of York. Audrey was nowhere to be seen. There was a blazing log fire crackling away and Donald sat down in his armchair close to the heat, with us not far away perched on a settee.

I thought to myself, if this were my house I'd be jumping up now to put the kettle on, but Donald merely tinkled a bell. Soon a housekeeper marched in with scones and homemade cakes laid out on a big tray. I will be in his position one day, I thought, my head spinning.

Donald put me at my ease, polite and charming and on his best behaviour. "Work hard," he told me, "and you can become a vet, too."

Absolutely, I thought, looking around the luxurious room. At that point in my life, it was one of the finest I had ever entered.

Only later did I find out that Audrey came from a wealthy shipping family, and that Donald's grand surroundings had little to do with his income from the surgery.

Although many of the stories shared in the pub or during our tea breaks turned up in Alf's books, when I first started visiting the practice no one really talked about his success in print. He was an intensely private man, although someone from London's literary world would occasionally contact him, a hint that Alf was more than just a vet. I also understood his desire for privacy and came to realise that he considered himself 99% vet and only 1% author. His writing aspirations were not shared with many, and certainly not with me. I wasn't working at the practice formally at this point and was 40 years his junior. Although I occasionally accompanied Jim to Alf's home for a cup of tea and saw "Herriot" typing in front of the television (he'd stop for a chat), I was just hoping to absorb everything I could at Kirkgate and become a vet. Jim remembers me enthusiastically cycling in bad weather to watch a post-mortem at the knacker's yard – not everyone's idea of a great day out, but I wouldn't have missed it for the world.

I was still a moody teenager, of course, and had my first girlfriend. But I was more than ready to work. Youngsters now are fortunate if they can manage to find a paper round or do some dog walking or babysitting to earn themselves a bit of money. Others can't find a job or, perhaps worse, get too much money from the bank of Mum and Dad. And unfortunately, the fingers of some children are rarely prised from today's multitude of gadgets. I've been really delighted, though, to see how *The Yorkshire Vet* has inspired many youngsters to take an interest in animals. My *Yorkshire Vet* colleague Julian Norton and I have had countless letters and many visits from children. Seven-year-old Max Stevens from Oxfordshire was just one. He wrote me a charming letter saying I had inspired him to be a vet. And not long ago Dylan, a little lad from Milton Keynes, asked his parents to bring him to Yorkshire to meet me – his idol, he said. The family came up for the weekend, visiting both the practice at Skeldale and the World of James Herriot visitor attraction.

At their age I had no idea what I would end up doing; I was too busy getting on with life. But then at 13, in 1970, my cosy world changed. There was a second world war prisoner-of-war camp near our village and Dad's friend Harold, also a keen poultry man, lived on the site. The pair decided to go into business together and managed to raise about £3,000 to buy the old camp, where they planned to rear chickens. Sadly, they were outbid by someone with a lot more money. Dad was really disappointed, but decided he still needed a change. Not long afterwards he took a job managing a new broiler-breeding site in a nearby village, which forced us to leave Manor Farm.

Ross Poultry, Dad's new employer, would play a key role in the industrialisation of the British poultry industry. According to Farmers Weekly, by 1978 the company commanded about 25% of the world market; but at the time, this meant little to me. Dad's new job meant we had to move house, although I could stay at the same secondary school in Thirsk and be with my friends. Granny and Grandad Wright weren't coming, which was sad, but we had a far more modern home with central heating to look forward to. I couldn't get over the decadence of it. We had come from a damp cottage with one fireplace in front of which we took our baths. Now we had warmth in every room and even fitted carpets. I loved it. I was also excited to make some new mates in this new village, and pleased to earn some money collecting eggs. I was paid about half a crown an hour, with time and a half on Saturdays and double time on Sundays. I did very nicely out of it and enjoyed the work, even on Christmas Day.

After collection, the eggs were taken to the hatchery to produce new chicks. Ultimately, the tiny birds would become broilers, which would alter Britain's mealtimes beyond recognition. Chicken was soon to become a key part of our diets instead of a rare luxury. I didn't know it then, but I was living in one of the heartlands of both the poultry and frozen food revolution. Not far away, two farming brothers called Guy and Eric Reed were to create a frozen chicken empire, Buxted Chickens, which became a household name.

I also didn't really understand that farming could be a real slog; from my ringside seat it still seemed fun. I just loved being in the Great Outdoors, playing football on a pitch we youngsters built by the side of the chicken houses. I topped up my egg income by driving tractors in the holidays on Guy Reed's huge arable farm. From the age of 15 or so, if I was off school at harvest time, I would start work around 8am and continue until midnight. I relished the camaraderie, the banter and the food. At around 10am we'd have our "lowance" in the fresh air – a bit of cake and apple pie, perhaps, or a scone. With all the money I was earning, I soon had enough to treat myself to a decent bicycle and fishing rod; I still have the rod and sometimes use it, even now.

Many of my friends at home and school loved the countryside, too, and had similar part-time jobs, some of them working with me. Those that didn't enjoy rural life so much would eventually drift away into other careers, often in the big cities. As I grew older I increasingly felt I was part of the land and the community, part of a team working outside to produce and protect what people needed for body and soul. There was something comforting about the work; its familiarity was soothing. It gave me security. But it was fun partly because I was still young and earning money without having to pay tax or the expenses grown-ups had to consider.

I gradually realised that farm work was not always easy, particularly in those days. My friends and clients, Jeanie and Steve Green, whom I've known since 1982, are well known to *Yorkshire Vet* viewers and own a small Thirsk farm visited by both Alf and Donald decades ago. Steve can remember Alf setting his puppy's leg in the 1940s. The little animal, a collie, fell from a bale of hay and broke it when chasing a cat.

Steve, who is now in his late 80s, was born on a farm near Whitby. In 1944, aged 15, he came with his parents to Thirsk (he left school at 13 to help his father) and has lived in the same farmhouse, on about 15 hectares (35 acres) of land, ever since. He started milking by hand when he was eight years old and with the help of technology was still at it in 2015, only stopping on the advice of doctors after a hernia operation. Viewers might recall the Greens' devastation when they had to sell the final six of their dairy herd; every cow was loved, had a name and was used to being handled. Now the cow houses where Rachel, Peanut and hundreds of other cows were milked over the years are empty, apart from a few cats' beds and some redundant equipment. The silence of the milking machinery and its connecting pipes is deafening. The Greens now rear about 10 calves, which are sold when they're around a year old, and also have a dog and several cats.

Jeanie, in her late 60s, was born about 250 yards from where she now lives and began learning how to farm – including how to drive a tractor – after marrying Steve in 1978. She often says, "There's nowt better than a good ol' cow."

If only more people agreed, instead of treating them as udders on legs: cows are not simply machines for producing milk. But Jeanie's heartfelt statement doesn't express the sheer amount of work involved in looking after farm animals. It's not for the faint-hearted: farmers are on call 24 hours a day and work from dawn until dark. The Greens have never been to York or London, let alone overseas, and the last time they had a day out – to Whitby – was more than 20 years ago. At least they no longer need to get up at 5am to milk cows or in the middle of the night for a calving. They now lie in – until 6.45am.

As a youngster I was surrounded by many people like Steve and Jeanie, countless hardworking role models and unusual characters, including farm worker William Willy, known far and wide as Billy Willy. He always seemed to wear the same clothes, and when he wasn't working he'd relax by smoking his clay pipe while leaning on his gate, waiting for passers-by to talk to. Just down the lane were the four Wilkinson brothers and their sister; another sister had married a farmer and moved to a neighbouring village. They were a kind churchgoing family who ran a farm. Despite their busy lives, they would often invite me in for a cup of tea and a slice of homemade cake. Their farm was their whole life; when they were growing up, their father said he was going to give them a holiday. They had to spend it painting the farm buildings. It was known for miles around as an immaculate homestead, with no weeds anywhere. Looking back, it's no surprise there were a lot of bachelors in the countryside, like my Uncle Richard and the egg man, George Barker. Such men had little time, and no doubt little energy once the work was done, to actively search for a wife. They frequently worked seven days a week and, of course, there was no internet dating back then.

My mother was another one who set a powerful example – toiling away endlessly without complaining. It's no wonder she was sometimes moody. She earned extra cash by helping out at dinner parties at a sprawling hall in a nearby village, and doing housework for Bertram Shackleton, who had the habits of an aristocrat. Some said he was related to Ernest Shackleton, the polar explorer. He owned a Bentley, had a butler and lived in a stylish, rambling house with an orchard. He seemed genuinely fond of my mother, who was trustworthy and discreet, and he took an interest in my progress at school. He was not the only one delighted when I got into veterinary college after all my work experience at 23 Kirkgate and hard work at school.

Not everything in my young life was rosy: I occasionally suffered from what I now think was depression. Throwing myself into my work helped, as I could avoid people and hide it from my parents, even though I felt sick or sluggish and didn't want to get up some mornings, let alone go to school. I was a hormonal teenager, of course, but sometimes I felt I wasn't good enough, perhaps because I knew I was going to take a path that would lead me further than my parents had travelled. Plus, Grandad Wright had died in 1970 and

Grandad Duncalf two years later. I missed them both, and their deaths made me ponder my parents' mortality.

Playing sport seemed to help my mindset, as did chatting to my teacher John Ward in the pub. As I was quiet anyway, none of the teachers seemed to latch on to the fact that I was sometimes low. I even visited the doctor, who was in his 60s and rather old-school; this was rural Yorkshire in the 1970s and mental health was rarely, if ever, discussed. He didn't know me well at all, and was not particularly sympathetic. Luckily, I came through this bleak episode unscathed. Looking back, I believe living in the countryside was a huge help. You could say, perhaps, that I had regular doses of ecotherapy without knowing what it was. All I knew was that being outside made me feel calmer and helped me find the mental energy to get on with my studies.

First time round, I managed two Bs and a C in my A Levels, in physics, chemistry and maths. Not bad, but not good enough to go to veterinary school in Liverpool. The university said it would consider taking me if I upped my grades and took biology. One of my teachers, Rod Jenkinson – later a good friend – stopped me one day and told me I was unlikely to get the results I needed.

"I can't see it Pete, I can't see it," he said, before disappearing down the corridor.

His words – which still ring in my ears today – made me all the more determined; I'd already set my heart on the city, mainly because it was in the north and reasonably close to home. I decided to retake my exams. I knew that I would have to work my socks off, or resign myself to never becoming a vet.

Meanwhile, my girlfriend left for university. Our relationship continued, although I now had more time to throw myself into my books. The following summer, 1976, with the help of some brilliant teachers, I retook physics and chemistry and sat biology too, which I had only been studying for six months. I soon had the results envelope in my hand. When I ripped it open I saw how well I had done: two As and a B. I blinked away tears of joy, hardly believing that this Yorkshire country bumpkin would soon be off to university; no one in my family had ever been. Although my parents were proud, they were also bemused. It was all so alien to them.

I was naturally keen to tell Donald and Alf my good news.

Donald pumped my hand vigorously. "Peter, you're joining a fantastic profession. I've had a lot of fun in my life; you will, too."

Alf was typically less effervescent, but I could see from his smile that he was pleased.

"Congratulations, Peter," he said. "You've worked hard; you deserve it."

Student vets letting off steam at a fancy-dress party. Peter is on the right.

CHAPTER 3

Losing Ratty

All six of us were drunk and had black makeup or masks on our faces; it seemed fitting for the joke we were about to play. We were about to break into the house next door, in the inner-city district of Toxteth in Liverpool. It was occupied by a group of young women whom we knew only slightly. Like us, they were students, but while we were hoping to become vets, they were taking physical education. We'd waved at them and said hello, but wanted to get to know them better, and for some silly reason thought that playing a practical joke on them would be the best way to make them notice us. Such is the idiocy of youth. In our intoxicated state we must have thought it would improve our chances if we dropped in, literally, from their attic.

From the table on the landing where (for reasons I will explain later) we ate our meals, we pulled ourselves up into the attic space above, shaking with suppressed giggles. It was about midnight. We pulled out a few bricks from the wall that divided our houses and were quickly through the girls' loft lid and inside their house, which was as large and decaying as our own. What now? We had no plan. We could hear a television and voices so knew they weren't asleep. I decided to turn on a vacuum cleaner that was close at hand. We then rushed to hide in the shadows, hearing one girl emerge to find what the noise was and see the machine gently humming. She turned it off, confused, and went back into her room.

Emboldened, we did the vacuum trick twice more. By then the girls were spooked, and a couple picked up carving knives before coming to investigate. This was the late 1970s, a time when the Yorkshire Ripper murders were still going on. We thought it best to make ourselves known and jumped out together like a bunch of idiotic magicians, spraying shaving foam over the screaming girls and their furniture. Their initial distress and a few choice and well-deserved words were quickly forgotten when they recognised us and burst into hysterical laughter. You could definitely say we'd broken the ice, so much so that my best friend Mark ended up marrying one of them, Louise.

I was enjoying my student days at this point, but the process of arriving in Liverpool and starting a new life had not been plain sailing. I had only the rather puzzled support of my family; Granny Wright struggled to understand my desire to be a vet.

"It'll be too hard work," she said, rightly linking the profession back then to the high number of small farms that rural vets still needed to visit, meaning heavy caseloads and little sleep. "You'll be working every day."

Granny Wright was not unlike many country folk of her era, believing office workers had the best jobs – inside and away from the weather, with the benefit of fixed hours. She wanted me to get a "good job", perhaps in a bank.

I saw her point. She had never had time for much relaxation and must have regularly gone to bed exhausted. Whist or domino drives, or an occasional dance in a village hall, were as good as it got for many women in Granny Wright's era, although she herself rarely did any of those. A lot of men, including in my own family, did make at least a weekly trip to the pub. Overall, though, the amount of leisure time many of us have now, and the variety of things we fill it with, were unheard of in my village community. I could easily see why my grandmother thought it was a silly idea going off to study veterinary medicine instead of getting a desk job. But the very idea filled me with horror. I could never live in a town or city long term; I knew I would wilt if I was too far from nature.

My parents had dropped me off with my large red trunk at the hall of residence where I'd be living. I was 19 and had felt a little sad as we drove away from the village that Sunday morning in 1976. But as we hit the main road, my principal feeling was a growing sense of anticipation about this new chapter in my life, a big step into the unknown. I barely noticed the Yorkshire countryside as we sped along, even though it was the last time I would see it for a while. My mind was focused on what I might find at the end of the journey: the studying, yes, but also new friends and parties, drinking, football and fun – shenanigans that Jim had raved about so often. I certainly wasn't pondering the crowds of knife-wielding muggers my Granny Duncalf was tearfully convinced I'd meet in the labyrinth of murky alleyways she imagined Liverpool to be made up of. I knew joyriders existed, but the only crime I'd really come across was the poaching of trout, and a man I knew being threatened by a hitchhiker with a knife. Norman, a former world champion wrestler, had calmly got out of the car, opened the passenger door, dragged the bloke out and then thrown him over a hedge.

Overall I'd led a sheltered life, its musical backdrop involving Abba, Neil Diamond and Ken Dodd rather than the Rolling Stones or Led Zeppelin. I went occasionally to York and Harrogate with my family, and Edinburgh for the day with school. My parents occasionally went to London, but I had never been. In Harrogate I'd once wondered how people were able to find their way among so many houses and streets; in York, the size of the river blew my mind. Now it was next stop Liverpool, of which I knew virtually nothing; I'd not even been there for an interview. I was looking forward to exploring, though, even if the Beatles and the Mersey were the limits of what I knew about the place.

Out-of-towners that we were, we asked for directions a few times on the outskirts of the big and grimy city before eventually getting to Sefton Park, from where it wasn't far to my hall of residence, Roscoe and Gladstone. The building was named after William Roscoe, a 19th-century anti-slavery campaigner, and the Liberal prime minister William Gladstone, whose father owned slaves in the British West Indies. In 2017 there were calls by some students to remove Gladstone from the building's name, but to me in the autumn of 1976, Roscoe and Gladstone was just the name of my new home. I had no real idea who either of these men were, given I'd been concentrating on maths and science, not history – Alf had studied English, French and Latin and was much better read than I was, but he wasn't in Liverpool to fill the gaps in my general knowl-edge – I just remember looking at a big brick block as a porter came out of his lodge to show me to my room. Block G, ground floor, room 3. I walked through the door and saw a window and a desk with a light to the right of it. There was also a shelf, a single bed, a washbasin and a toilet. I was told there was a shower block and kitchen somewhere nearby.

It's slightly embarrassing to recall, but my first thoughts were not about the quality of the facilities, but about security. No one will get me in here, I remember thinking. That might seem a little pathetic, but coming from the countryside to live in Liverpool was a major transition. It took me a while to adjust. I'd been pleased to spot Brook House, a rather drab Victorian pub nearby, but Granny Duncalf's words about potential muggers were starting to ring in my ears. I was just glad my accommodation was secure and pleased to see a grassed courtyard outside the window: at least there was some greenery. My parents were happy with the set-up and helped me unpack my trunk and the food Granny Duncalf had sent for me. Her fruitcakes would soon become legendary among my university friends.

I had been away from home a few times before, to my girlfriend's and on hostelling trips along the Pennine Way, but never this far. Now I was about to be marooned from everyone and everything I loved, long before the arrival of mobile phones and the internet. It felt as though I was on another planet. Luckily, my usual fear of failing kicked in. This will be an adventure, I told myself.

My mother was upset, but trying to hide it. My father was calm. They told me to look after myself.

"Watch your possessions," Mam reminded me. "Put your wallet deep inside your pocket. And make sure it's a pocket with a zip," she added. "Be careful when you're out late at night. Watch the traffic."

She had tears in her eyes and was still giving me advice as they climbed in the car and drove quickly away with me watching. I felt a swell of love for my parents, quickly followed by a surge of excitement at the thought that I'd be a veterinary surgeon in five years, if I worked hard enough.

I was still shy, but not as retiring as I had been. Anyway, I knew I needed to make some friends if I was to thrive in this alien metropolis. A lad in the room opposite told me he was studying zoology. He seemed decent. I can get on with him, I thought. A guy down the corridor seemed pleasant too. Shortly afterwards I discovered that a would-be vet was in a room upstairs. I found the door wide open on my third attempt at meeting him.

Knocking, I peered in, saying, "I understand you're doing the veterinary course."

As we shook hands, I was pleased to see he was wearing an anorak, just like me. As Mark Robinson from Cheshire made me a cup of tea and told me about himself, neither of us had any idea we'd be best friends for more than three decades. I'd be his best man (and he'd be mine); with some other friends I'd even spend a few days with him and his wife during their honeymoon in Tunisia. Mark's dad was a vet and he'd been to private school. He played rugby and was used to living away from home.

I'd met a few pupils at secondary school who at some point had been privately educated, but I hadn't really registered what that meant. They were just other pupils. My student days at Liverpool were the first opportunity I would really get to meet so many people from so many different backgrounds. Around half the intake in 1976 was from private schools, but that was irrelevant. Even though

Mark's upbringing was quite different to mine, it didn't matter: we just clicked.

Nowadays I have friends who are multimillionaires, as well as friends with little money. It really is the person that matters to me. I have always been proud of my humble beginnings and feel privileged to have had my rural upbringing. Even after some time in Liverpool, I still felt a bit like a country mouse, with Mark my worldly-wise cousin; but it was a relief that he seemed to know some of the ropes and wasn't at all arrogant. He was normal. If he's typical of the students in my year, it won't be too bad, I thought to myself during those early days.

On that first Sunday afternoon, in that bare little room and in our unfashionable anoraks, Mark and I began a treasured and unbreakable friendship. We moved on to chat and laugh in the refectory, where afternoon tea was served, meeting other freshers along with students in their second or third years. Nowadays, there are often 200 or more veterinary students in one intake, but in Liverpool that autumn there were around only 50. I was starting to relax and enjoy being with so many people who wanted to be vets. We had a lot in common, and soon they would feel like family. But if I was feeling less out of my depth, I was still nervous about going to lectures for the first time.

On Monday morning we were to report to the veterinary faculty on the university campus in the city centre, a couple of miles from our halls. We had to work out which bus to go on and from which bus stop – something I'd never done, as there was only one bus to Thirsk from my village. You got on it or you didn't. At least I already had an ally in Mark and we could work it all out together. There was a tangible air of excitement among the students on the bus during that first trip into what was then a run-down city. It was no longer a thriving port at the heart of the British empire, and was clearly not in its heyday. I was ecstatic when, 32 years later, Liverpool became European Capital of Culture, which gave an incredible boost to its coffers, infrastructure and reputation. Not long ago I visited the city with my son. In my student days I wouldn't have dared venture alone to the area around Albert Dock, but now it's all done up and buzzing; it's fantastic to see.

The bus full of students weaved its way along Smithdown Road, past pubs and takeaways, butchers' shops, Kwiksave and Tesco. These were names I'd heard of but was not bosom buddies with. I was delighted to see a Chinese takeaway. After finding out I'd been accepted for Liverpool, Alf and Jim had taken me to York for a celebratory meal in the Willow, a popular Chinese restaurant. I was only used to traditional British fare and was panic-stricken as duck, noodles, ribs and rice appeared on the table. Jim says he'll never forget the horror on my face, but I was persuaded to tuck in and expand my dietary repertoire. I was an immediate convert, and Chinese food was to be a regular part of my life in Liverpool and beyond.

As we passed the Chinese the road opened up. I saw a big round-about, and straight ahead a huge skyscraper: Entwistle Heights was 22 storeys high. How horrible it looked! It was the tallest building I'd ever seen. How could people enjoy being crammed in there? I didn't understand then that it had been built to try to cure some of the social problems caused by crumbling 19th-century hovels, which had no doubt been grand family homes once. These tower blocks also replaced buildings destroyed in the war. Residents probably lived there out of necessity, not choice, just as my family had worked on the land: that was what they knew, and what had been on offer.

That Liverpool tower block was eventually pulled down, but when I was there it was a familiar landmark. Soon our bus went past the Roman Catholic cathedral, known as "Paddy's Wigwam". I hated it on sight. It looked like a massive concrete nose cone belonging to a space-bound rocket. However, slowly but surely it grew on me; whenever I saw it, I knew I was getting close to the university, where my mind would be stuffed with facts and challenged by fiercely bright tutors posing one medical dilemma after another.

Within two or three months, some of us began walking instead of taking the bus, while rather cheekily continuing to claim our travel grants. My tuition was free and I got a full grant to live on. I was grateful for the fact that my education was being funded by the government; I'm even more so now, given the debt so many students get into to pay for their education.

That first term wasn't easy. I was missing my girlfriend, I was homesick and I was suffering from culture shock. I drank pasteurised milk for the first time in Liverpool, having always had fresh milk straight from the cow at home. I was coping, though, and was starting to enjoy myself: the coursework, the new friends and the social life. But when my girlfriend suddenly dumped me, it knocked me back. Mark and some other friends, particularly Andy Routh, Nick Winn, Steve Spencer and Mike McKnight (later we'd become the Attic Gang of Six) helped me through my misery, taking my mind off it with trips to the pub. Mark and I also played a lot of backgammon, and I threw myself into sport and work. My fear of failure was always lurking in the background and I knew I was surrounded by some very bright people. Plus, I'd not been accepted first time around and knew I'd be expected to work to a very high standard. We all realised that we could be thrown off the course if we failed too many of our end-of-year exams. Any we did fail we would have to resit in the summer holidays. Several students had to do that. Others had to leave because they were unable to keep up.

During our five years in Liverpool, we covered many topics with many tutors. Professor King took us for animal husbandry, a subject that looked at the care and breeding of livestock. He was probably in his 60s and always wore a three-piece suit, his hair slicked back, never out of place. Unlike some lecturers, he didn't go out with the students socially, but I liked his manner and concise delivery. He would sometimes say: "We men cannot know what it's like to give birth – but imagine defecating a turnip." The corners of his mouth would turn up a little as we laughed. This was during our third and hardest year, when microbiology, pathology and parasitology were also on the agenda. By then, some students were on antidepressants as they struggled to cope. Only in the fourth year would we start looking in depth at actual medical conditions; there was so much basic knowledge to soak up first – the foundations needed to be laid before any of the brickwork. Nick, Mark and I always worked extremely hard, whereas Steve and Andy didn't seem to do as much; they appeared to take it all in with ease. They'd sometimes bob off to the pub while I'd sit with their notes to make sure I'd properly understood a lecture.

One of my favourite teachers was Mr Beasley. He was bald and had a large head and a big nose, so we gave him the rather unimaginative nickname "Beaky Beasley". He taught us about fleas, lice and worms (his pet subject) in the university's world-renowned School of Tropical Medicine, established with a donation of £350 in 1898 by the shipping magnate Sir Alfred Lewis Jones. Liverpool was a major seafaring port then, and the massive amount of trade it did with other countries, including parts of Africa, had many benefits, not least of which was the abundance of jobs. A major downside, though, was the rising number of tropical diseases appearing in Britain, many of which came into the country through ports like Liverpool. The number of people admitted to hospital with unusual illnesses soared, and Sir Alfred wanted them investigated. In 1915 a four-storey purpose-built facility was erected for the job, but it was used as a military hospital during the first world war; research into some of these exotic diseases only got underway in 1920.

I sat in this important, solid-looking building and felt some of the weight of history on my shoulders. We were learning more than the basics; some of the experts there were doing major research. Later I found out that Joseph Everett Dutton, who discovered a parasite linked to sleeping sickness, and Wolferstan Thomas, who developed the first effective treatment for this disease, had both worked at the School. They were pioneers, and I was soaking up their marvellous achievements.

In 1921 Sir Alfred stumped up more cash for the school's first research laboratory abroad, in Sierra Leone. Its discoveries in West Africa included finding out that a particular kind of black fly was responsible for transmitting parasitic worms to humans, worms that cause a very nasty disease called river blindness. In 2016, more than 129 million people were treated for this illness in Africa. It was clear to me as I sat listening to Mr Beasley that the School of Tropical Medicine was doing essential work of international importance that had an impact on the health of millions.

We also heard about the research that had been done with former British soldiers who'd been prisoners of the Japanese in the Far East during the war. They had picked up some gruesome diseases in captivity. Mr Beasley was passionate about his unusual subject, and would beam as he regaled us with ghastly tales of parasites. We sat enthralled, listening intently to one of the few men on the planet who loved creatures most people would squirm to even think about. He taught us how to recognise many different organisms we didn't know existed, and the life cycles of different species, many of which had to be learnt off by heart.

One particular parasite would take me by surprise in the early 1980s, by which time I was fully qualified and working back in Yorkshire. While I was doing a routine cat spay (neutering a female), the poor creature, just six months old, died on the operating table – every vet's worst nightmare. I remember Donald being very sympathetic and reminding me things don't always go according to plan. These kind words were well meant, but had little impact on my despair.

When I told the owner, he agreed to let me try to make some sense of his pet's death, so I examined her body. Opening up the cat, I discovered a phenomenal number of lungworm lesions. This was highly unusual, and the sheer quantity helped to explain why she had died. I've never seen such an invasion of worms in a cat's lungs since. I sent a sample off to Cambridge University and was told the specimen was preserved for veterinary students to study. My *Yorkshire Vet* colleague Julian Norton went to Cambridge; maybe he even saw the sample himself. I felt a little better knowing I hadn't done anything wrong during the operation, and that at least something good had come from the worms and the far-too-early death of their host. I imagined Beaky Beasley with a knowing smile on his face.

I've now spayed thousands of dogs and cats, but my first was at university with two or three students to a table as the teacher went round checking our work. I was lucky, as I'd already seen the operation done many times in Thirsk during my work experience. In the holidays in my final year at Liverpool, Alf, Donald and Jim even let me carry out the procedure myself, under supervision. When I landed my first job after graduation, in Luton, I was already well used to what had by then become one of the mainstays of the veterinary profession.

But this was only one of many procedures I came to know. As we progressed through our five years at Liverpool, my university classmates and I watched and performed myriad operations and dealt with more real cases, starting with the dissection of stray dogs that had been euthanased by the RSPCA and donated for research.

We got to know the anatomy of all kinds of animals quite intimately. However, it's fair to say that over the years, I've worked on some body parts far more often than others. In *The Yorkshire Vet*, I'm thought of as the go-to man for removing the testicles of dogs, cats and countless other creatures. I'm even known by some as "Mr Testicle". Sometimes, our daily list on the surgery whiteboard contains nothing but castrations.

A couple of years ago, three lads on bikes recognised me while I was out walking in the woods with my boxer dog Alf, not long before he died. Knowing my reputation, they jokingly stopped to ask why the dog still had his testicles. It was a fair enough question, a well-meaning attempt to highlight my apparent hypocrisy given the number of screen hours that have involved my destruction of the male dog's genitalia. Alf still had his testicles because he was virtually asexual, exploring both male and female dogs with licks and affection but never attempting to do anything else. If Alf's testosterone levels had made him hypersexed or aggressive, like the hundreds of head-butting lambs or overly raunchy donkeys and stallions I've often had to deal with, I would have lopped off his testicles too.

In my Liverpool days, someone would occasionally throw a dog's testicle across the classroom while we were dissecting bodies. Sometimes one would smack into the side of my face, ruining my concentration, but when I looked up the usual suspects appeared totally engrossed in their canine cadavers.

At university we did a lot of work comparing anatomies, looking at differences and similarities between various species. We'd had hundreds of lectures by then, with subjects ranging from the structure of bones and muscles to how embryos evolve and where fish come from. We were pleased when a brand-new veterinary hospital was built next door to the faculty in our first couple of years, as this allowed us to put our knowledge into practice through regular consultations with the public and their pets. Unfortunately, the work was not always uplifting. Liverpool had a lot of stray dogs at the time, many of which had distemper, a viral and highly infectious disease. The symptoms were coughing, vomiting and diarrhoea, often followed by seizures, paralysis and death. We had to euthanase a lot of animals. I found this very sad, especially as there was a vaccine available; but even dogs with owners were not always inoculated. No doubt many families didn't believe their own pet would be affected.

After a year in halls of residence I moved into the semi-detached house in Toxteth, where I played our attic trick with Mark and the rest of our gang. We stayed there until our fifth and final year, when all veterinary students were required to move to the university's Leahurst Campus in the Wirral countryside to learn more about treating horses and practise more surgery. Our Toxteth house was sadly ransacked and set on fire in the riots of 1981, just after we had finished our studies and left Liverpool, but our memories of the place are fond. When we weren't studying or playing sport, we were laughing and partying. Living together firmly cemented the bond between the six of us.

It was a house of horrors in some ways, right next to a cemetery and with a garden full of old bike frames and bottles; but it was huge, and perfect for parties. We had the top two floors and six bedrooms, each with a lock on the door. The bathroom was horrific and there was initially no kitchen, but being practical chaps who would soon be performing intricate and lifesaving operations, such a little problem was easily overcome. We created a basic kitchen on the top floor out of a storeroom that had a sink, water tank and heater. We boxed in the tank, bought a cheap cooker and fridge and ate our meals on the landing, cooking in pairs for all six of us according to a rota.

Initially, the menus were quite inventive as we grappled with new recipes and cooking techniques. I'd arrived with my mother's recipe for Yorkshire puddings and perfect roast beef. Steve made superb pavlovas, while Andy, a fellow Yorkshireman, went for value for money. He spent hours preparing braised heart and pigs' trotters that just ended up being moved from one side of our plates to the other.

Soon the effort involved became too much for us, and as the novelty of cooking wore off, the quality of our evening meals went rapidly downhill. Nick's cheap faggots were so vile we ended up splattering them against the landing wall when his back was turned. Pork steaks and Angel Delight were soon on the menu all too often.

The bottom floor and cellar were rented to about 15 people who were all on benefits, including a woman with a baby. There were often curious smells wafting around that I had no clue about, never having smelt cannabis before. I didn't dare tell Granny Duncalf about the tenants below, as she'd probably never have slept again. One lad even used an old wooden door in the garden to practise throwing a large knife at.

We got on well with these neighbours at first, but as time went on they increasingly made fun of us for being students, and the relationship began to sour. I'm wise enough now to see things more from their point of view; we were receiving government grants to learn, and we were having fun, knowing we'd have good careers at the end of it. I don't think the downstairs occupants had much to look forward to. Sometimes we found our car tyres slashed or our only television gone from Steve's locked room, his door prised open with a crowbar. Of course, we didn't know for sure that the thief was from the group below; but we were suspicious, as it happened a few times – always when we were out.

When we did have a television, we would crowd around the crackly old set on Sunday nights to enjoy *All Creatures Great and Small*, although we could only get a half-decent picture. Everyone in Britain seemed to be watching the programme and even now, when I hear that lovely and evocative theme tune, the hairs on the back of my neck stand up. Seeing Donald and Alf on screen as Siegfried and James, and all the characters from home, made me feel extremely proud, and a little homesick. My friends knew about my links with Alf and Donald, but we didn't talk about it much. After all, we too were becoming vets, and had our own fun and games going on; in many ways, we were living the books ourselves. But I do remember some students in the year above doing a comedy sketch for our faculty about the TV programme. The Drovers Arms, a pub mentioned in the Herriot books, rudely became the Turd and Paper and James Herriot was renamed James Hairybit.

During university rag week in our second year, many of us took part in a long procession through the city on a float. My friends and I stood next to a big papier-mache cow we'd made in our Toxteth house. We also made a sign for the lorry that said "It Shouldn't Happen To A Vet", the title of the second Herriot book. With our white coats and stethoscopes around our necks, we had a raucous and memorable trip through the Liverpool streets. So I couldn't really get away from my roots even if I wanted to; Alf and Donald and my beloved Yorkshire were still a part of my life in the city through the TV programme and, of course, I saw them regularly in the practice when I went home. I had the best of both worlds, going back to Yorkshire regularly during holidays, sometimes working on a stud farm and gaining other experience that was helpful with my university course.

The only thing missing from my life in Liverpool was an animal to love – one that I didn't have to dissect. Then one night in the pub, when I was still living in the halls of residence, I bumped into a fellow veterinary student called Madeline Forsyth. She was a couple of years ahead of me and would later become a colleague in Thirsk. She said she had some pet rats and promised to give me one as a present. The next day, nursing a hangover, I found a rat in a cage outside my door.

That was the start of my lovely relationship with Ratty. When we moved into the house in Toxteth the following year, he came too, and lived in my room. I loved holding him and talking to him, and often fed him morsels of Granny Duncalf's shortbread. He also enjoyed a drop of Ribena in his water bottle. So you can imagine my dismay when one evening I returned home and unlocked my room to find the cage door open and Ratty gone.

It was like Spot the rabbit all over again. There were a lot of holes in the floor of my room, so I pulled up several boards before turning the house upside down, my ear to the ground as I listened for scratching. I still hadn't fully resigned myself to the loss of my pet when I sat down to our house Christmas dinner a week later, just before going home for the holidays.

As we were about to eat, a large gift was pushed towards me.

"This'll cheer you up," somebody said.

I pulled off the paper, then lifted the lid of the cardboard box inside and gazed down at a rat, which stared right back at me. It took me a second or two to realise it was Ratty.

My five housemates were by now laughing, tears rolling down

their faces as they saw my confused but delighted expression. They explained how they had gone on a top-secret mission to kidnap Ratty from my locked room as part of an elaborate practical joke; while I'd been out with my new girlfriend, they'd tied some bed sheets together, opened a window and lowered Andy, the lightest, from the top floor to my room, where I'd left a window open. He'd placed Ratty in a plastic tub, and Mark had kept him in his room in a trunk.

I couldn't be annoyed, partly because it would be seen as weakness, but partly because I did see the funny side. Besides, I was so glad to see Ratty again. He was none the worse for his ordeal and lived for another year or so, eating many more pieces of Granny's shortbread before passing away. I would go on to have many more pets after Ratty, but wonderful as they all were, none have ever been involved in an airborne stunt outside my bedroom window. Ratty will always be the champion as far as daredevil deeds go.

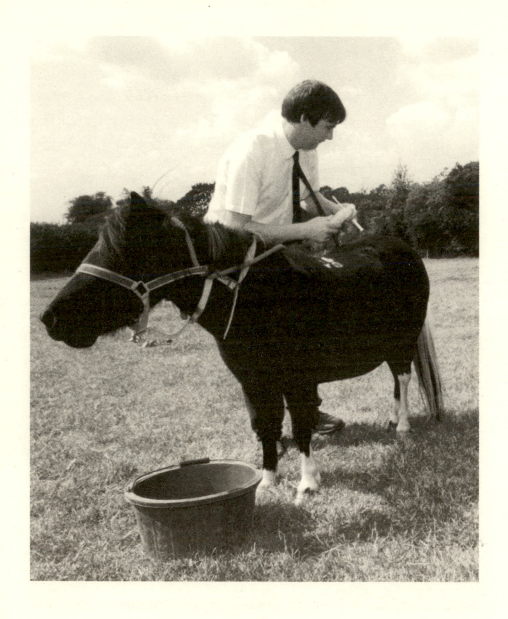

Peter treating a friend's Shetland pony.

CHAPTER 4

A German Shepherd
in a Tower Block

I was still a Yorkshire country bumpkin, despite five years in Liverpool, when I went up a tower block for the first time. It was late on a Saturday night in Luton in 1981, a few months after I had qualified as a vet. The area was seedy, and I was scared as I scrambled up the graffiti-covered stairs with only dim lights to guide me. I had zero interest in any views on offer, as I was on my way to visit a German Shepherd dog with gastroenteritis.

At Kirkgate, Donald always drummed into his staff: "Number one rule – you must attend!"

I wasn't sure he would have wanted to attend here, though. He always said he loved night work; the only issue we younger vets had was that he never did any.

When I arrived at the flat in Luton, slightly out of breath, the youngish couple who opened the door were drunk and possibly on drugs: neither were coherent. Both they and their squalid home, with its overflowing ashtrays and cheap furniture, stank of cigarette smoke. I experienced culture shock again; I'd seen some of this kind of life as a student through the tenants who lived downstairs, but I'd never witnessed it in the real world outside. The big dog lying calmly on the threadbare carpet was a friendly enough animal, despite being under the weather. Rightly or wrongly, I found him less intimidating than his owners or the building, despite his size and his breed's potential for aggression. The chaos in which he lived is still clear in my mind. When I was done, I almost flew back down the stairs and drove away quickly, glad to leave, but also depressed about the way the couple and their pet lived. It was a million miles from my innocent and idyllic upbringing.

In 2016 in an online discussion, Luton was named the worst place in the UK. The most popular comment seemed to sum up the mood: "Luton. Horrible town. Horrible inhabitants. Thank God there are three motorway junctions, two railway stations and an airport that can be used for a swift exit."

Rather harsh, I thought, although I admit I didn't live there long, and didn't want to stay. I lasted just a few months because the lure of home was too strong. But even though it was a challenging location for my first job, I still have some good memories of my time there, including treating gorgeous Jersey cows in the countryside nearby. I also had some lovely colleagues. And there was Morris, an adorable tabby cat. He'd been unwanted as a kitten, but I couldn't wait to see him when I came home from work; I loved to hear his little feet running to the door to meet me as I climbed the stairs to my flat.

I was quite lonely in the evenings, with little social life to speak of. During the week I was too busy working 11-hour days, and at weekends I usually drove to see the girlfriend I'd had since university. But Morris was my constant friend and companion. When people come to me for help with the animals they have talked to, stroked and cuddled for years, I completely understand the immense joy and pain associated with having, then losing, something so close. To lose a pet is to be bereaved. I've seen grown men cry over hamsters, and there's nothing wrong with that. I'm old enough to have seen several of my own pets die; I've put some to sleep myself. But enjoying them, and knowing you've given them a lovely life, outweighs the sorrow of their passing.

As I've mentioned, Lin and I recently lost our second boxer, Alf. *Yorkshire Vet* viewers might remember seeing him in some of the early episodes. One day, he suddenly collapsed on his way home from his daily walk in the woods. Within an hour, this key member of the family, liked by people who usually show no interest in dogs, was gone, despite my frantic efforts to save him. We still had the belligerent, stroppy and arthritic cat Mary, but her health had never been good and soon after Alf's death I had to put her to sleep. The house felt empty, soulless even, as our two children had by then already flown the nest. We struggled to cope, especially Lin, who has always been more popular than me with our pets; she has a wonderful rapport with them. To them, she's both Mum and mate, and I understand that. In Luton, Morris heard everything about my life; he really seemed to listen and, if he was passing judgement, I was blissfully unaware. It was Morris the tabby who helped me navigate the transition from university to the big wide world.

To say Luton was my first job is not strictly true. Straight after university I briefly worked in Essex for a lovely vet called Jerry Kew. I'd done a placement with him during my university studies and was grateful when he gave me a temporary job after graduation while I looked for a suitable long-term position. I soon read about a vacancy in a mixed practice in Luton, meaning lots of large animal work as well as treating pets. I'd never been to the town before, but knew Vauxhall cars were made there and that the comedian Eric Morecambe supported the football team. More importantly, I knew Luton was surrounded by beautiful countryside, which would allow me to do the farm work I was really interested in tackling.

In the interview, I was excited to see how progressive the practice seemed. It used computers, unusual in 1981, and had its own laboratory with a full-time technician. The vets could analyse blood samples on site. They even did their own histology, a process of studying animal tissue; a retired pathologist who'd worked in a nearby hospital came in once a week. He'd take the sections of tissue we'd collected, such as from the breast of a dog we suspected had cancer, and make a diagnosis on the premises. Even now, it's rare to have such expertise so close at hand. The Luton practice also had nurses, including a rather scary but excellent head nurse. She taught me the value of organisation and I saw just how much vets benefit from being surrounded by good staff. There was also an accountant, but he, perhaps naturally, was always trying to cut costs, so most of us didn't like him.

All in all, it was nothing like Thirsk. There, Joan Snelling had become an excellent secretary but was not a trained nurse, even though she sometimes helped out during operations. She remembers early on being asked for the first time about a cat spay, and having to find a vet to explain to her what one was. Gradually, as the nature of the business changed, she learnt how to sterilise instruments and how to keep an eye on anaesthetic levels during operations. As for Kirkgate's banking system, for a long time it centred on a tankard on the mantelpiece that would often be overflowing with notes, coins and cheques. (The tankard is now on display in the Herriot visitor attraction.) Joan – a real diamond who could turn her hand to anything – painstakingly wrote out invoices by hand for years.

The Luton practice was owned by two likeable vets, Peter Kemble and Owen Pinney. They had two assistants and were looking for number three. I was taken on in no small part because of my solid grounding in Yorkshire. I'd regularly calved cows and lambs, castrated bulls and done routine operations under supervision; many of my peers hadn't had nearly as much experience as I had. I could hit the ground running, and even felt confident enough to ask for more money in my interview. I was soon living in Dunstable, a market town just outside Luton, in a large flat above one of the three branches of the practice.

I mostly worked in the main branch in Luton. Not long afterwards, I moved to a flat above the branch in the town of Harpenden. I soon began to lose weight, as there was little time to eat: the hours were intense, and I usually survived the day on just a bowl of porridge that I'd forced down for breakfast. There was no time for lunch. I was also an absent-minded cook, once forgetting to turn off a pan of mince before I left for work. Luckily, the practice staff noticed smoke coming from upstairs and called the fire brigade, but the walls of my home were black and the smell of smoke lingered for weeks.

After that, I increasingly ate takeaways, or dined alone at Chinese and Indian restaurants; not surprisingly, I soon put on the weight I'd lost. While I was used to Chinese food, I was still relatively new to curries, although I'd eaten a few with Alf and Jim in Darlington. I had some sympathy with a man I overheard in my local Indian one evening. His girlfriend asked him for recommendations, as she'd never eaten Indian food before. Under her gaze and intense questioning he began to flounder, finally admitting he'd only eaten it once himself.

"All I remember is a wet flannel and a big crisp," he confessed.

He meant, of course, a hot towel to wipe his hands on, and a poppadom. I snorted with stifled laughter, but was thankful I wasn't the only one uncertain about Indian menus.

At least I was feeling surer about how my career was progressing. I was tired, but not too worried about the long hours. A bigger problem was that the pull of Yorkshire was strong. My family and friends were never far from my thoughts, so I was pleased to be invited on a walking holiday in the Highlands of Scotland with Jim and three other mates from home. It was spring, 1982, and there were few of the midges that annoy summertime visitors.

It was a brilliant trip, except for the little issue of us biting off more than we could chew. We'd wanted to climb Ladhar Bheinn, the highest mountain in the Knoydart region. The wild scenery was enchanting, but there'd been some snow, and after a while putting one foot in front of the other became really hard work. Two in our group decided to turn back early on but I, Jim and Paul – a former dairy herd manager who'd become a travelling salesman and taken up smoking – pushed on. We were still a long way from the peak when Paul suddenly declared himself exhausted. Only when his arms and legs began to flail wildly did we realise he was on the verge of collapse; his blood sugar must have dropped dangerously low. Jim fed him several marmalade sandwiches and we supported his not inconsiderable weight to a cottage on the shores of Loch

Hourn. A fisherman ferried us across the water while we watched the sun set behind the snow-capped mountain we'd not managed to climb. The end wasn't quite what we had planned, but the view was some consolation.

This trip into the wilderness, which naturally included conversations about Kirkgate and Thirsk, made me think even more about my roots. I began to see Luton as a step on the ladder; I realised that Yorkshire would be my ultimate destination. As it turned out, the ladder was a short one, as I soon had a call from Jim. A young vet was leaving the practice: was I interested in his job?

I was mentally packing my suitcase before I'd got off the phone. It wasn't long before I was walking up Kirkgate's three steps and through its red door, just as I'd done many times before. But now I was coming back in a far more important role. I was elated and, as usual, also a little apprehensive at the thought of not being able to live up to what was expected of me. The fact that I'm still at the practice says something about how it all went.

Just as in Luton, I had to work hard and was often on call, sometimes working continuously for two weeks without a day off. Donald was now working three days a week and Alf two, given their respective ages, and neither did nights. I didn't mind, though, because nearly every patient and client I saw sharpened my skills or taught me new things. The long days and antisocial hours did become trickier when I got married and started a family, but in my first few years back in Yorkshire I had no responsibilities other than work – and Morris, of course, although sadly he vanished one day when he was about two. I never found out what happened to him. Any pet owner will understand that your best mate suddenly vanishing is one of the hardest things to cope with.

Alf and Donald were two very different personalities, but somehow they complemented each other. I saw with increasing clarity how over the decades Alf must have learnt to bite his tongue, or simply to ignore Donald's hare-brained ideas. Alf was a logical, calming and reassuring influence who tended to keep any worries to himself. He also found humour in his work, as his books so clearly show. He would sometimes pretend to look into a crystal ball when a difficult call came in and say, "Ahhhh, yessss, I see a young vet going out on this one. Yessss, yessss, a young vet." Then he'd grin and one of the assistants would have to set off to castrate a batch of wild and uncooperative young bulls, or do some other equally demanding task; all the same, it was impossible to be annoyed with him.

Donald was a trickier character to deal with. He was an excellent vet and always looking to take the practice forward and innovate, getting many of his ideas from the Veterinary Record, a magazine for vets.

"Look at this, boys. Shall we try it?" he'd say.

He was even more eccentric than his portrayal suggested in the Herriot books. Once Donald and Jim were doing a routine cat spay when the patient suddenly stopped breathing and died without warning. It was probably the early 1970s and they were using ether, a very unpredictable anaesthetic; it could be difficult to get the dose right. Donald immediately sprang into action, grabbing the dead cat and running outside. He began whirling it around, something vets and farmers often do with newborn lambs to encourage them to take their first breath. But Donald, energetic as ever, swung the cat with too much vigour. It suddenly slipped from his hand and shot through the air into the garden of the Royal British Legion next door, hitting a man who let out a stream of expletives. Sadly, the cat's flight had no effect on its breathing: it remained dead.

Donald always worried about finances. One day I heard him say, "Alfred, we don't need all these staff. I could run this practice single-handedly!"

Alf nodded as if he were pondering the matter, but was noncommittal, probably thinking his partner's concerns would soon pass – like virtually all the others. Not long afterwards came a day when our colleague Madeline (who'd given Ratty to me at university) was away on holiday and I was on a farm visit. Jim was also out and Alf was on a day off. Donald, who was then about 70, arrived at 9am to find no sign of Joan Snelling, our secretary; it turned out she was ill and at home. There was already a queue outside and I can imagine Donald unlocking the front door while politely greeting the clients and urging them to take a seat inside. To the customers he was always the epitome of charm and grace, although the amount of work that lay ahead must have seemed gargantuan. To make matters worse, as soon as he stepped through the door the telephone started to ring, and didn't stop.

Later, when we looked at the day book from that morning, it showed that his usual scrawl became less legible and more frantic with each entry. More and more people came through the door, and to top it off, a man called Johnny Moss brought in his lanky Afghan hound, Branston. We all knew Branston, who was roughly 70cm tall and a not-inconsiderable 30kg. He disliked vets with a passion and was difficult to handle on the best of days. This day was already not a good one for Donald, who must have been fretting as he failed, miserably, to multitask. A bystander watching Branston being examined would have probably seen the blurry arms and legs of the increasingly hysterical vet and Johnny Moss shooting off in all directions, the massive dog climbing all over them and the furniture.

The day got worse. There were more farm calls and the arrival of several pets that needed minor operations – and there was no one to do any of it but Donald. Then came a call about a foal. Donald was a horse expert and always keen to treat them himself. Hearing about the poor creature's torn eyelid but knowing he could do nothing about it was the final straw.

Alf was relaxing at home when the phone rang.

"Alfred! Alfred! Get your bloody self down here as quick as you can! There's not a soul here, not a bloody soul! I'm all by myself!"

Then the line went dead. Alf dutifully drove in to work. There was no mention again of Donald running the practice single-handedly.

Donald was a generous man. He grew Christmas trees that he sold during the festive period and always gave one to me. One year, when our children were young, Lin even found three that he'd left in our garden. I heard countless tales of his generosity, including how he'd bought a new pig for a family after he'd failed to save their original animal and realised they couldn't afford another. But he could also become too involved in people's lives. I remember him bluntly advising me to "drop like a hot brick" the woman I'd started going out with at university, because he didn't think two vets could work as a couple. We did split up eventually, but it took us a while.

Donald involved himself in my personal life in other ways, too.

He loathed the steel-toed shoes I wore to work and once asked me if I could wear something different. I didn't want to, because the shoes I had protected my feet from the various hooves I didn't always manage to avoid. But I often caught him staring at my footwear (he loved shoes, once buying himself 24 pairs in the same style in Marks & Spencer), so it was no surprise when one birthday he gave me a new pair. What was surprising was how hideous they were — slip-ons with plastic soles and plastic uppers. Donald had previously bought some for Jim, who was more polite (or less fashion-conscious) than I was; he actually wore them. They lasted about a week, his feet sweating and smelling the entire time.

By this point I had met my future wife Lin, who worked nearby at a dental practice. She took one look at Donald's gift and marched the shoes back to the shop to swap them. When Donald's name came up in conversation the manageress said he'd recently been barred, as he'd slapped her colleague's bottom. Although I'm not excusing his behaviour, I do think context is important. He was born in 1911 and grew up in a very different time. He was virtually a man when all British women were finally given the right to vote. Nowadays, Donald would undoubtedly face criticism from gender equality campaigns but, as I've said, his was a different era. Over the years, I'm sure many members of the opposite sex found him utterly charming and debonair, even when he was well into his 60s and 70s. In the Herriot books, Siegfried (Donald) regularly makes ladies swoon and, of course, author Alf knew Donald very well. Now it's common to greet a woman you know with a peck on the cheek but in his day, he was the only man I saw do so. I know several women who still talk about him and his sometimes wandering hands with affection and no rancour; but Lin and I had some sympathy for the shop employee, and I was pleased he'd been banned from the premises: it meant I was less likely to receive any more ludicrous loafers.

Donald (like Siegfried) believed absolutely that whatever he thought was right, and could rarely, if ever, be persuaded otherwise – even when he was obviously wrong. He might change his mind much later and contradict himself, but it was usually pointless trying to put across your own point of view while he was holding forth. Most, if not all, of the young vets were at some point summoned by him to the dispensary, full of shelves crammed with bottles and powders with names like "Oxygas for Udder Ill" and "Universal Cattle Medicine". There he would dispense his words of wisdom or, just as often, his criticism.

One morning I called at the surgery on my way home for breakfast and a wash, having spent half the night out on a farm helping a calving cow, when Donald summoned me for a little talk. He immediately told me to follow him into the tiny dispensary. Perhaps I'm getting a pay rise, I thought.

"Where's your tie?" said Donald, who always wore one himself, even if his usual neckwear of choice was a careworn, grey-greenish thing that hung limply around his neck. He was prone to colds, and when he felt poorly wore a red spotted handkerchief around his neck. I believe he'd been wearing the same one for decades.

Alf used to say: "He's got his spotted hanky on; he's going to be off tomorrow."

Whatever he had on, though, he was still my boss, and he'd caught me out. "My tie's at home," I replied.

"You're a disgrace to the profession!" he roared. "Get it on before you come back to work!"

I didn't dare say I'd stripped off to put my arm inside a cow.

I found out later that Donald had told off other colleagues about their attire. *Yorkshire Vet* viewers may wonder why Julian and I always wear ties; it's just one of Donald's legacies.

Not long after I returned to Thirsk, Donald was knocked over by a motorcycle and broke his leg. We were all worried, not least because he was in his 70s; but the doctor said the bone would heal, though he'd need a cast and crutches for a while. Despite Donald's difficulties walking, he still insisted on doing a few visits. Joan remembers him visiting her horse, despite her advising him to send another vet. The animal accidentally stood on Donald's foot − the one attached to the injured leg. She said he somehow managed not to swear, although he must have been in agony.

Other visits were less eventful, although some of the journeys to get there were memorable. Donald had an automatic car, so managed to keep driving, somehow laying his injured leg across the passenger seat. He refused to be beaten, although he did realise that occasionally he needed some help. He wouldn't be able to vaccinate a horse, say, while hobbling around on crutches, so he'd take me along to perform the necessary task while he watched. I would have to climb into the back of his car like some dignitary and we'd set off, picking up speed as we hurtled down the country lanes. The Herriot books refer to Siegfried as an unorthodox driver. Similarly, Donald was always erratic behind the wheel, frequently squashing flies on the inside of the windscreen with his hands while using his elbows to steer. Sometimes I'd shut my eyes as he veered across the road to the honking horn of a passing car.

"Peter, did you know those people?" he'd shout from the front. "They seemed keen to attract our attention."

One market Monday, with his leg still injured, Donald had arrived back in Thirsk after a farm visit with me when he suddenly announced he wanted some new car-seat covers. I hadn't even formed a reply before he was driving onto the car-free square, a heaving mass of stalls, stallholders and shoppers. For Donald the matter was simple: he wanted some seat covers and he was going to have them – even if he had to drive where he shouldn't. He squeezed here and dodged there, weaving in and out of the shocked pedestrians, including many farmers and other Kirkgate clients. I was almost on the floor of the car, hiding out of embarrassment, but Donald was oblivious, focused on the mission at hand. He suddenly spotted a stall selling covers and jerked to a halt as close as he could get.

"Go on, Peter," he yelled. "Go and buy me some!"

I scrambled out, cheeks burning, and left Donald sitting impatiently behind the wheel while I quickly found some brown covers that would go with his brown car seats. I just wanted the ordeal to be over.

"They're no bloody good," he barked. "What's the point of brown seat covers with my black Labradors?"

Often with Donald, you just didn't know what he wanted.

Later, still cringeing, I told Alf what had happened.

"That's typical," he laughed. "Whatever you do with Donald, you won't win."

Sometimes Donald's angry driving and erratic behaviour had expensive consequences. Once, when driving his brand-new car – just three days old – at the top of a hill near his home, he stopped and got out to remonstrate with a farmer working on a track. Donald's view was that he was digging out too much soil, which would therefore need a greater quantity of expensive stone on top; and it was only a farm track. As he purposefully strode down the steep incline, he didn't notice the farmer's eyes, transfixed on what was playing out behind him. The gleaming blue car was slowly gathering pace down the hill, then turned two somersaults and came to rest against a sturdy oak tree. Donald had forgotten to apply the handbrake.

Alf was undoubtedly quieter than Donald, but was the source of just as many stories. One of my favourites also involves driving. It's related to a client from the upper echelons of society: a woman known as Lady Anne. She was mad about horses, especially racehorses, and would always give her highly-strung charges their supper personally at around 11pm, even when she was very old and could hardly walk. She and Alf were about the same age. One day in the early 1980s (when both of them were pensioners), he was driving back from lunch for afternoon surgery when he saw her. She was dawdling along in her beaten-up old car, full of straw and horse feed. Alf was never a fast driver and didn't take risks; but he didn't want to be late for work, so he decided to overtake her in his Peugeot. She must have been offended – or in the mood for danger – because she immediately hit the accelerator and kept pace with Alf as he tried to pass. There they were, two cars neck-and-neck, with the occupants' white hair gleaming in the sunlight as they hurtled along the single carriageway towards Thirsk.

Alf's face was ashen when he arrived at work a few minutes later and told us about his ordeal. "If anything had been coming the other way, we would have had it," he gasped.

At work even now, I'm regularly reminded of Alf's stories: there are a few signed Herriot books in the staffroom upstairs which, for whatever reason, were never collected by their owners. They lie in a tall display cabinet that used to stand in our office at 23 Kirkgate, but now leans against a wall in the purpose-built Skeldale Veterinary Centre, where we moved in 1996. It naturally came with us, but not knowing where to put it we carried it upstairs, intending to move it later on. We never did. In the 1980s, when Alf was at the height of his fame and when *All Creatures Great and Small* was almost compulsory TV viewing, there were often signed books in the cabinet. I was regularly astounded to see hordes of people inside and outside the surgery, all hoping to have a chat with Alf and get his autograph.

All in all, working with him at that time was not unlike having a rock star in our midst, albeit one who avoided the limelight and didn't enjoy being the centre of attention. But with people coming from as far away as Japan, Australia and America to meet their literary hero, and with Alf being a gentleman who couldn't abide rudeness, he didn't want to let his fans down. He was so unassuming; Lin once told me that she'd been saying "good morning" to him in Thirsk for at least a couple of years before she realised he was James Herriot.

Of course, some fans couldn't visit the practice and wrote to him instead. He received huge numbers of letters, most of them charming, some of them quirky. I remember one from an American man saying the end of the world was nigh. As luck would have it, the chap was planning to build a spacecraft, and said that Alf was one of the lucky few to have been allocated a place.

Outwardly, he was unruffled by all the attention and seemed calm and composed. I only ever saw him really agitated once – the day Madeline and I decided we'd play an April Fool's Day trick on him. It was 1983, and my job included being in charge of welfare and hygiene at a turkey factory. I'd recently had to certify that a consignment of parson's noses (from the tail of the bird) was fit for human consumption, and could be sent on its way to Togo in West Africa. I had to show the meat was free of a bacteria called *Pasteurella tularensis*, often shortened to *P. tularensis*, before it could be shipped, as it can cause a potentially fatal disease. It was all new to me – Togo included – and I also had no idea who specifically wanted to eat parson's noses there. Regardless, this gave me an idea for a joke.

A few days later it was April 1st and Madeline and I found ourselves in the surgery with time on our hands and the desire to cause mischief. Alf, by now with a worldwide reputation as James Herriot, was due in. How could we catch him out? We decided that because one of his weak spots was his determination to keep his home life well away from the spotlight, we would use that.

We quickly concocted a letter from a fictitious Doncaster tour operator called A1 Tours. It said something like this:

Dear Mr Wight,

We run a successful business taking tourists of many nationalities, particularly Americans, to places of interest in Yorkshire. We would be most appreciative if on the last Wednesday of every month you and your wife would kindly provide refreshments at your home for a coachload of our clients. Please let us know by return what time would be convenient and the type of catering you can offer.

We signed the letter from the managing director, a Mr P. Tularensis, and then we put it in an envelope addressed to Alf and popped it on his desk.

Alf soon walked into the room and Madeline and I watched as he opened his mail. His face immediately dropped as he read our few lines.

"Oh, my God," he said. "Oh, my God." As Madeline and I exercised all our reserves of self-control in our efforts not to laugh, Alf picked up the telephone and asked for directory enquiries. "I'd like the number for a Mr P. Tularensis, please." He spelt it out. Nothing. "No one of that name? What about A1 Tours, Doncaster?" Again, nothing.

He put the phone down, looking cross. I'd never seen him so flustered.

"This is unbelievable! Look at this. What do they think I am?" he said, almost bursting with indignation as he showed us our letter. He was already peering out of the window, perhaps imagining gaggles of camera-wielding tourists padding up to the door, expecting Mr Herriot and his wife to have the kettle on and the homemade cake sliced, with a tour to follow. "For my wife to have to provide them with refreshments. It's just not on!" he blurted.

He was about to say more when I interrupted. "I know that name, P. Tularensis."

"Do you, Pete? Do you? Can we get hold of them?"

"I don't know," I said slowly. "But I've just been involved with a *tularensis*. I've sent some parson's noses to Togo. I had to certify they were free from *pasteurella*. *Pasteurella tularensis*."

The penny still didn't drop. "How am I going to get hold of them?

I will have to write to these people!"

That's when Madeline and I finally took pity on him. "What's the date today?" we said.

There was a pause. "April 1st. Oh, my God. Oh, my God. You buggers!" The three of us fell about laughing. "You really had me there."

I was confident enough to play this joke on Alf because I was beginning to talk to him as an equal, even though he was my boss and mentor. It hadn't been like that when I'd first started at the practice on work experience as a shy teenager. Back then I was in awe of him, even though I realised early on that he would have a big impact on my life. Some of that influence was far more subtle than teaching me basic veterinary skills. When he took me out with him on calls he would often play classical music in the car, which I wasn't used to at all. We would drive along listening to a tape. Later, I learnt it was usually Beethoven or Mozart. Hearing this music, and surrounded by Yorkshire's allure, there were times when I experienced such intense emotion I couldn't have put it into words. In essence, I felt life couldn't get any better.

Sometimes Alf would say: "Peter, let's stop and stretch our legs."

He'd park the car and we'd go for a walk with his dogs. I remember Hector, a feisty, blind Jack Russell, and Dan, a black Labrador who'd initially belonged to Jim. Regular haunts were some woods near Ampleforth College after we'd visited its dairy herd, and around Sutton Bank. From about 300 metres above sea level, you can look down on Garbutt Woods and also Gormire Lake, formed during the last ice age. Some say it's bottomless. Alf thought it was the best view in England, and I'm inclined to agree. Years later, his ashes would be scattered there.

We'd only walk for about twenty minutes here, but I loved these interludes. We'd watch the dogs running around and chat about football, one of our favourite subjects, or Alf would ask about my university course and what I thought about life in Liverpool. He was always interested. Sometimes we just walked, enjoying the peace and tranquillity, but there were never any awkward silences. There were no mobile phones to disturb us, either; in those days the only contact with the outside world was a telephone kiosk at the top of Sutton Bank. I always felt a little sad when Alf stopped and called Kirkgate to ask if there was any more work near us; it meant our walk was over. But when we hit the road again, often to another farm job, and with more classical music to accompany our journey, I couldn't have been more thrilled. A trip to Sutton Bank now, more than 20 years after Alf's death, still makes me feel nostalgic for the walks and chats we shared in my youth.

As I've already mentioned, I feel nostalgia more frequently these days. I suppose it's all part of the cycle of life. One of my favourite things to look at in the old cabinet at Skeldale (the one with the signed Herriot books) is a chloroform mask we at one time used to administer anaesthetic to horses. Now consigned to the history books, the mask is basically a canvas nosebag that was strapped onto a horse's head. At the mouth end is a pocket with a zip containing a sponge. The zip would be opened and the chloroform poured in. When the sponge had soaked it up, the horse would breathe in the vapours and fall unconscious. If this all sounds rather simple, it wasn't. As Alf always said, "You have to catch your patient first."

I would usually accompany Donald to help with horse castrations, being the "man on the head" with the chloroform mask while he did the surgery. Such events were unpredictable: once we had the horse in our clutches and the mask on, we would never quite know how long the animal would take to go down, or even if or where it would go down. Sometimes there would be a phase of excitement and the horse would go marauding across the fields, crashing through hedges before being overcome by the vapours. You never knew where you'd end up doing the surgery, and I'd have a strong sense of trepidation before any procedure involving the mask. The animal could wake up too soon, or not wake up at all. I was apprehensive about ensuring the dosage was right, partly because I didn't feel I had enough information or experience. At university we didn't talk about the masks much, as chloroform had pretty much had its day by the time I started studying; I've even seen it mentioned in texts from the 1860s. But Kirkgate was still using it more than a century later, because Alf and Donald were so used to it.

In Essex and Luton we'd used a drug called immobilon instead, which is easier to use but very dangerous for humans. Vets have even been killed with it by accidentally scratching themselves with a loaded needle without the antidote to hand; and in 1995, a British vet was sentenced to life in prison for murdering his wife with the drug, then freed in 1998 after a suicide note was found. If chloroform was not as obviously frightening, we still had to watch our patients carefully, sometimes needing to unzip the nosebag and pour more liquid onto the sponge. No one wants to be kicked by a horse, as one kick can be as fatal as the deadliest drug. Luckily, we Kirkgate vets all used the chloroform mask regularly and survived.

Horses are unpredictable, with or without chloroform, just as Donald was. Alf once told me a tale involving a man called Hilton Denby who lived in a village just below the Hambleton Hills. It's likely that Donald, who had his own horses and hounds, went hunting with him. Alf and Donald were at Mr Denby's premises one day, preparing to knock a horse out for a procedure. It was usual practice, and common sense, to warn the client that the procedure could be lethal. The liquid had already been poured into the mask when Alf whispered to Donald, "You've warned Hilton about the risk of chloroform, yes?"

Donald abruptly turned to Mr Denby, standing a few yards away, and shouted: "Hilton, you do realise your horse is probably going to die, don't you?"

Luckily it lived, although I'm not sure the two vets were ever invited back.

In the cabinet near the horse mask are two other items from the past which, when combined, can make me feel rather anxious. One is a small cardboard box that houses a small tube used for testing for anthrax, one of many notifiable diseases – vets who find it have a duty to inform the authorities. The other item is an old-fashioned microscope that could identify it. Most members of the public probably think of anthrax in the context of biological warfare, but vets sometimes have to deal with it. This bacterium is potentially fatal for humans and animals, as I know from personal experience. It is transmitted by breathing in anthrax spores, which can also get into the body through broken skin, and vets are at risk from it through their contact with infected animals or their products. Anthrax spores can also exist in a dormant form in soil, plants and water, and are hard to destroy, although the occasional outbreak in Britain is closely monitored by the authorities to minimise its spread.

Whenever an animal died suddenly and inexplicably, the farmer would have to call us, and we'd tell him not to move the carcass before we got there. We'd rush over and take a small sample of blood from the animal's ear and test it on behalf of the government. Alf always said the knacker's yard vehicle was the "vets' failure van", as the knacker's men dealt with the dead stock we weren't able to save. We were, naturally, rather reluctant to contact them, as it meant dwelling on what had gone wrong.

One evening we had a rare call from the knacker's yard themselves. One of the symptoms of anthrax is an enlarged spleen, and the yard was concerned enough by this particular cow's body to get in touch. Panicking, Donald quickly sent me out to investigate, as he hated any situation involving the authorities. I checked the carcass, saw a huge spleen and took a blood sample before dashing back to the surgery. Under our microscope I could see there were some bacterium chains with purple capsules that looked like anthrax. I was very nervous but still uncertain, so I rang the Ministry of Agriculture, Fisheries and Food. Within half an hour it had sent out its own veterinary officer to see my sample, but he too scratched his head, unable to draw any firmer conclusions. He called out yet another vet, an anthrax specialist, who decided it was a bacterium from the same family that had caused the animal's sudden death from septicaemia; as it was a slightly different shape, it wasn't anthrax. There were sighs of relief all round.

I was reminded of this episode recently when I read an article about the disease rearing its ugly head in Siberia. An outbreak in 2016 killed a 12-year-old nomadic boy and made around 100 people ill. More than 2,300 reindeer died. Officials apparently thought the epidemic started when a heatwave thawed permafrost, and with it the infected corpse of a long-dead reindeer, which released bacteria into the air. As I was reading I glanced warily at our old microscope and anthrax tube and wondered if the disease could become yet another consequence of global warming – something else to worry about.

A quick look at a bronze bust of Donald on top of the cabinet put a smile back on my face. It was made by vicar and sculptor Toddy Hoare and I recall stumbling across him and Donald in a consulting room, the vet sitting still and quiet for once while he posed for the artist. A few weeks later the finished sculpture appeared, the right ear sticking out a little: an accurate portrayal if ever there was one. Looking at the face of my old boss staring down at me, I decided to put the world's problems aside for the evening. I got up, turned out the lights and went home.

Miss Cecilia Constance Grome-Merilees, and her Dachshund Dapple.

CHAPTER 5

The Glamour Grams

My life at Kirkgate as a newly qualified vet settled down, and as the seasons rolled past I enjoyed immersing myself in the rhythm and pace of the job, back in the heart of the countryside I knew and loved so well. It wasn't long before I was building up close relationships with some of the regular visitors to the practice. I have always liked continuity with clients, where people see the same vet each time. It's why I avoid employing part-timers, as they are not always available when a patient really needs them.

This custom of having a particular vet for a particular client stems in large part from the 1980s, when Alf and Donald assigned me to treat the pets of several elderly ladies. They usually lived alone, apart from their dogs and cats. These pets were so precious to them that they would want me to look at every cough, scratch or hiccup. Sometimes we'd spot one of them coming down the street before they actually arrived. If it was Alf who saw them, his eyes would suddenly widen and he'd say, "Peter, it's one of your Glamour Grams" – his adaptation of the word stripogram. We'd look out of the window to see an elderly lady climbing the steps with a reluctant dog. Calling them Glamour Grams was perhaps a little politically incorrect, but Alf never meant any harm by it.

One of my favourite old ladies was Cecilia Constance Grome-Merrilees. This lovely name conjured up in my mind a society lady from a bygone era, but it was also a little long, so I just called her Miss Merrilees. She was a petite woman with a gentle, reserved nature and a cut-glass English accent. Rumour had it she'd been a nanny to a minor member of the royal family, and I think she'd moved up to Yorkshire from the south of England. She rented an idyllic but ramshackle cottage on the Newburgh Priory Estate, not far from Thirsk, and drove to the surgery in her battered old Ford Fiesta. Her arrival was always signposted by the sound of a car screeching to a halt, and the sight of the diminutive driver peering over the steering wheel. Miss Merrilees wore a hat that was fixed with a hat pin, and she usually had on a long coat that reminded me of Agatha Christie's Miss Marple; she had that kind of amateur detective air about her. I wouldn't have been at all surprised if she'd been out solving a murder or two in between visits to the vet.

Her two dachshunds were her pride and joy. One was a touch vicious, the other very much so, and I had to be careful they didn't take my fingers off. I often visited the dogs at home and they would bark relentlessly.

"Oh, you two are so naughty!" Miss Merrilees would tell them, with great affection.

The dogs' ailments were usually quite trivial: they would have fleas or need a minor procedure, such as having their anal glands emptied. Dogs use the glands to secrete a liquid to mark their territory. It's foul-smelling, and although owners can do the procedure themselves, many understandably choose to pay some-one else to do it; as the Kennel Club says, it's not the stuff of dinner party conversations. Job done, I would then watch Miss Merrilees gently cradling the dogs in her arms like babies, as though butter wouldn't melt in their mouths.

I tended to be in that area a lot, and if I passed her cottage on my way back to Thirsk I sometimes called in for a coffee and a chat. There was much more time back then for vets to be part of the community, out and about talking to people. The very kind Miss Merrilees became a friend, and when my daughter was born, she gave me a beautiful silk hand-smocked dress for her. It had originally been made for one of the children she'd nannied, and we still treasure it. Her friendship was a reminder that being a vet is a great equaliser; you must learn to mix with people from across the social and political spectrums – from peers of the realm to those who live in shacks.

Although Miss Merrilees clearly had good taste and possessed a few dusty antiques, she was not obviously wealthy. She often talked about her plans to leave what little she had to a children's home in York; her money, such as it was, would come from the sale of four original pencil etchings by Ernest Shepard, the *Winnie the Pooh* illustrator. At some time in the past, Miss Merrilees had apparently known him, and his signed and framed pictures hung on her walls. As she got older and realised it was perhaps time to have them valued, she contacted a reputable London auction house and an employee came to her home. He took them away, telling her he would pass them on to someone with greater knowledge.

She never saw the drawings again. She even hired a law firm, but they couldn't track them down. I remember her showing me a few letters from her solicitor. It was an upsetting episode, although she was the stiff-upper-lip type and wouldn't show emotion while I was around. Eventually, Miss Merrilees ran out of steam and cash to continue looking for the drawings. It was a real shame to think that someone had just kept them, or pocketed the money from their sale. A couple of years ago London's *Evening Standard* reported that an original drawing of Christopher Robin and Winnie the Pooh playing "poohsticks" sold for more than £300,000. I don't know if it was one of the four that had been on Miss Merrilees' walls, but it certainly shows their value.

Another of my Glamour Grams in the 1980s was Peggy Brown, a formidable character who taught me a lot. She lived in a run-down cottage in Harome, a village near Helmsley. She was tall and well built with a ruddy complexion and messy hair, and often wore a pork-pie hat perched on top of her head. She was well educated; I heard years later that she'd had a pilot's licence in the 1930s, so her family must have had some money. Now I wonder if she'd known the world-famous pilot Amy Johnson from Hull, the first woman to fly solo from Britain to Australia and an early member of the gliding club at Sutton Bank.

Miss Brown, probably in her 70s when I met her, lived alone, apart from half a dozen cocker spaniels. She was a hoarder, always surrounded by boxes of books, newspapers and magazines. On her feet were dirty, worn shoes, and she usually wore a large grubby mac with various buttons missing. Rather than sew more on, she would just tie the coat in the middle with a piece of twine. Her legs were often ulcerated and covered in bandages. Appearances can be deceptive, though: she was one of the most fascinating people I've ever met. I got to know her well through her dogs and her interest in trying to treat her pets with natural remedies. She was interested in environmental issues (she might have even lectured on them) so I usually learnt something new when we talked. I would adjust my treatment according to her knowledge and ideas. Treating her pets was a key lesson in my efforts to understand what a client wants – something I always urge my staff to do.

Miss Brown didn't always get things right. For one thing, she was against vaccinations and I sometimes had to do a lot of persuading before she gave in. But in many ways she was well ahead of her time. She firmly believed we were poisoning ourselves with the chemicals we put on our crops. It was no surprise to me that she loved pyrethrum plants, which produce a natural insecticide. She would buy huge white buckets of a powder made from them, then douse her dogs with it to try to protect them from fleas. I remember the powder being scattered all over her cottage, too; she thought it much better to have this mess than deal with man-made chemicals. One particular group of such chemicals, called organophosphates, were also used to kill fleas, and as a young vet I sometimes used them. But Miss Brown banned me from using them on her dogs and, in hindsight, she was right to do so: they turned out to be poisonous.

In fact, organophosphates are frightening chemicals. They can disrupt the use of our muscles and were used in chemical weapons in the second world war. Sarin – the gas released into the underground system in Tokyo in 1995 in a terror attack – is the best-known organophosphate-based weapon. These chemicals have also been used in farming, but here again problems have been detected. Some research suggests they have negative effects on the environment and human and animal health. In 2016 the *Guardian* reported that at least 500 farmers across the UK were left with serious health problems after using organophosphate-based chemicals to protect their sheep against parasites. Worldwide, these substances are said to kill thousands of people every year.

Hindsight is a wonderful thing. Few people in the 1980s paid much heed to people like Miss Brown or her environmentalist friend, a forthright widower called Major Scatchard. He had his own organic vegetable plot and believed everything was being poisoned by the chemicals we use on crops. He often talked about potential problems arising from things like using too much plastic, or the fumes from cars. The major gave me a 12-page document he'd typed out, which I still have. It talks about "man's relentless pursuit of wealth from the manipulation of more and more chemicals designed to change life in a way which will accelerate the illusion of better things to come". He thought too many chemicals would eventually lead to people, animals and birds becoming ill, and would also damage trees and plants. I thought some of what he said made little sense; I certainly didn't see him as a prophet. Now, though, I'm not so sure, given the sorry state of much of our environment. Some of the substances he hated were eventually banned, but there are many suspect materials still in our midst.

I was happy to know people like the Glamour Grams and Major Scatchard because it made my job as a vet so interesting. I was always meeting colourful characters or finding myself in unexpected situations, even when I was supposed to be off duty. Once I was even called into action while watching a football match between Arsenal and my own team, Middlesbrough. It was on a well-earned day off and I was looking forward to enjoying the atmosphere of the FA Cup, which was tense from the very start of our home match at the Riverside Stadium. Arsenal scored, and a deafening cheer went up from the away fans. It made me and thousands of other Middlesbrough fans want to weep; but little did I know that it had led to an entirely different situation behind the scenes.

The first I heard about it was via an announcement on the public address system a few minutes later. "If there's a veterinary surgeon here today, can they please go to the back of the south stand."

I forgot the game and quickly made my way outside, remembering that this was where mounted police officers gathered to segregate home and away fans before and after matches. The horses they ride have to deal with thousands of rowdy people, so are carefully chosen for character, fitness and ability. They are brave and extremely well trained, and usually perform brilliantly – not just at football matches, but also at New Year's Eve celebrations, riots and royal weddings. I've heard of minor issues, like the horse that became separated from its rider during a royal celebration and was seen running across the forecourt at Buckingham Palace, but major problems are rare.

I arrived at the back of the stand to see a horse with blood pumping out of one of his front legs. When Arsenal supporters had cheered their goal, the poor creature had been so startled that he'd reared up and put a leg through the windscreen of a police car. The vet who usually attended these matches was away and I had no medical equipment in my car, but I managed to calm the horse and stem his bleeding, applying pressure with some police bandages. Luckily, the wound wasn't too serious and I found out later that my temporary treatment had saved the day until he could be stitched up. I went back into the match and saw Middlesbrough lose, afterwards wondering why I'd bothered returning to the stands. Success isn't everything, though, and I wouldn't alter my allegiance for all the tea in China.

By this time I was well used to treating horses, and many other species. I still came across situations I found difficult (that being the nature of the job), but it was rare for me to be given a task I wasn't keen to attempt. It did happen from time to time, though, and the day I was chosen to treat an elephant must count as one of the most unusual. Nowadays, circuses in Britain rarely have exotic creatures and a special licence is needed to use wild animals. In fact, the government has announced that their use in travelling circuses will be banned from 2020 – something supported by the British Veterinary Association, which believes, quite rightly, that the welfare needs of wild animals cannot be met within a travelling circus. But in my early years as a qualified vet, the situation was less clear-cut.

I remember Alf checking the day book that morning, then looking into his "crystal ball" with a grin before telling me my destiny was to visit a circus elephant with an infected tail. I was apprehensive, to say the least. I'd never even met an elephant before, never mind treated one, and knew I could be crushed, kicked or thrown. Or maybe, my imagination now running wild, I would be savagely beaten with the animal's substantial trunk. But off I went.

I needn't have worried. The wretched animal's tail was oozing pus and layers of skin were coming off, but she was calm and docile. Elephants are intelligent, with the largest brain of any land animal, and I felt she knew I was trying to help her. I moved closer and, keeping an eye out for her massive feet just inches from mine, injected a bottle of penicillin behind her ear with a 5cm (2in) needle to get through her substantial skin. The tail soon healed.

It was a memorable string to add to my bow, although I haven't had call to treat another elephant since. That's fine by me; they're better off in the wild.

At this time, one of my regular jobs was tending a dairy herd at Ampleforth College, which is run by Benedictine monks. Unlike the circus elephant, it was a challenge I always welcomed. I ended up going there most weeks for several years in the 1980s. My Granny (Annie) Wright, the one I'd lived next door to as a child, had died the year after I returned to Yorkshire, but I often thought of her when I visited the college, as she'd come from a farming family in the village. The boys from the school would often call round at their home to enjoy a drink and a singsong with her father.

I first became familiar with the herd when visiting with Alf as a veterinary student. After calving, cows are often ill with milk fever (a calcium deficiency), and need a big bottle of the mineral injected into a vein. I often held the bottle for Alf while he worked. Later, I got to know the 250 or so animals and farm workers on my solo visits. I'd see about 30 cows each time, brought before me by a brusque cowman called John Dawson, who had an amazing knowledge of cattle. He called me Uncle Wright (sometimes Uncle Herriot), despite being about 15 years older than me. He wanted to create proper records for the first time at Ampleforth, to find out exactly when the animals were most likely to calve, and wanted to make sure the cows had one baby per year; this would ultimately improve the herd's efficiency and lead to more profit from milk sales. As I've mentioned, some of this delicious liquid went to the Harbour

Bar in Scarborough, my childhood ice-cream haunt. Other milk was used to make yoghurt, and I often went home from Ampleforth with a big pot.

My visits to this gorgeous spot soon became one of my favourite parts of the week. I enjoyed going there whatever the weather or season, even though I sometimes had to get up early. Testing for TB, for example, had to be done during milking time, which meant getting there for around 4.30am. Sometimes I didn't have time for a proper breakfast, but there were consolations in store. I'd take along a flask of black tea; I didn't bother with any milk because I knew that at the college I could just dip my cup into the tank that was quickly filling up with delicious, fresh liquid from the cows. Sometimes I'd be sipping my tea while the sun came up. It seemed no drink could ever have tasted better.

I was used to seeing John the cowman at Ampleforth, so was surprised to see him appear in Kirkgate one day. He was holding a basket and looked flustered and upset. He pulled away a blanket and revealed a very poorly-looking Jasper, a ginger farm cat that he'd hit while driving a tractor. He'd once seen Jasper with a mouse under each paw and another in his mouth, although the cat hadn't seemed to know quite what to do next. Now, though, it looked like his promising career as a mouse-catcher was over.

With tears in his eyes, John, usually aloof and undemonstrative, said, "Uncle Wright, I don't care what it costs. I want this cat put right."

Luckily we fixed Jasper's broken pelvis, and within a month he was back on his feet. I always saw John in a different light after that. He would never have admitted he was fond of an ordinary farm cat, but he was like many people – even no-nonsense farmers – who spend so much time with some animals that they begin to see them as loyal friends. Later, John became the estate manager of Ampleforth College, and cowman Allen Harrison, from the Yorkshire Dales, was brought in. He was phenomenal with the cows, a gentle soul totally dedicated to their wellbeing.

Donald had been friendly with the abbot at Ampleforth, but the only monk I knew was Allen's tall, thin and thoughtful friend Father Bede, a former quantity surveyor. Now he's a parish priest who does a lot of retreat work, helping people find quiet in a busy, noisy and confusing world. What is this life for? And how should I live? These are just two of the questions Father Bede and his colleagues encourage Ampleforth visitors to ponder. Despite his godly life and 5am morning prayers, though, he's still a Leeds United supporter, like Allen. Father Bede even followed his team around Europe. It always brought a smile to my face, imagining him in his habit and Leeds scarf at an away game in Germany, although he probably just dressed in civvies for the occasion. Once I went with them both to Middlesbrough to watch our two teams play. There was Father Bede, calm, collected and quiet, and then there was Allen and me. Leeds won, and I came away feeling miserable; but the day was exemplary of a different kind of football etiquette, a kind I've never forgotten.

Good things often come to an end, and in 2000 I was disconsolate when I had to stop working at Ampleforth: the college sold its herd. Falling milk prices, which had hit so many farmers, affected the monks, too, and they decided the cows had to go. The end of the

Ampleforth era was not the only demoralising incident I faced, although I was getting older and becoming at least a little wiser. I was beginning to realise that you have to accept life's changes.

Seeing Joan Snelling, the former secretary at Kirkgate and Skeldale, recently reminded me of this truth. She's in her 70s now; I'm in my 60s. We are both grandparents with greying hair, and sometimes it's hard to understand where all the years went. Joan began working full time at the practice as a teenager because her parents couldn't afford to continue paying for her education. She was one of Jim's classmates; her headmaster, a friend of Alf's, had recommended her for secretarial work. On her first day at work she turned up at 8am, as instructed, to find the front door locked. She waited for an hour before everyone else arrived. Only then was she told a spare key had been in the window box all along. It wasn't the only thing she wasn't told. One day an unfamiliar vet turned up at the practice. She didn't even know he worked there; he'd been away testing cows for TB for a month.

I'm glad Joan hung around. By the time I came along for my first day of work experience, she was already a vital member of staff in a small but busy practice. She was increasingly helping to deal with pets and their owners, as that side of the business had started to grow. This was partly because Jim had bought a small anaesthetic machine, which meant cats and dogs no longer had to go all the way to a vet in Darlington for operations. The increasing work with pets came as farm work started to dwindle. Kirkgate worked with around 90 dairy farms in the late 1960s; Skeldale now has barely a handful. As Jim says, a farmer with 200 dairy cows would struggle to turn a profit today, but in times past a man with 20 cows could make a decent living. Many small farms have been swallowed up

Left: Me in 1962, aged 6.
Below: In primary school with my classmates.

Above: My former bosses Donald Sinclair (Siegfried Farnon) on crutches and Alf Wight (James Herriot) with Donald's brother Brian (Tristan). **Below:** Alf Wight signing his book for a fan with Joan Snelling on the phone at 23 Kirkgate in 1978; she worked for the surgery for more than 40 years. **Opposite:** Hilda Whitaker, a retired teacher who lived in a flat above the surgery, watching Alf sign books with Donald.

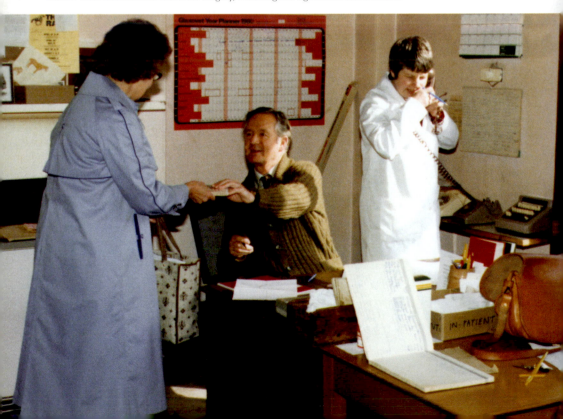

Above: Me with longstanding colleagues Tim Yates and Jim Wight, with a statue of Alf in the garden at 23 Kirkgate – now the World of James Herriot visitor attraction. **Below left:** The typewriter that Alf wrote his Herriot books on in front of the TV in his living room! **Below right:** With Tim and Jim in the kitchen, which used to be the operating theatre. **Opposite:** With Jim looking at the day book, where calls were recorded. We're standing in the dispensary, where Donald would chastise many a young vet, Jim and me included!

This page: Donald (Siegfried) with his beloved black Labrador Sam. He had many black Labradors and once told me off for buying brown seat covers for his car – they wouldn't match the dog hair! **Opposite:** The bronze bust of Donald in my practice. The sculptor was the Reverend Toddy Hoare, who captured an excellent likeness.

This page: Our old phone at the World of James Herriot. It was initially three digits and is now six. **Opposite:** Joan Snelling, our secretary for 44 years from July 1959 to June 2003. She was in Jim's class at school.

This page: L to R, colleagues Tim Yates, Andrew Barrett, me and Jim Wight, looking out of the window of the office at 23 Kirkgate. **Opposite:** Taken in 2018, Jim (with his dog, Cleo), Tim, me and Joan. All grey now – but when we get together the years seem to melt away…

Opposite, clockwise from top left: Oxygas was used to treat *'Udder Ill'* or *'Chill In The Bag'* (now known as mastitis) and also *'Milk Fever'* (now known as hypocalcaemia).

Old vet equipment at my practice in Thirsk. These old remedies have been kept at Skeldale as a reminder of medicines used in a bygone era.

The old microscope from 23 Kirkgate used during the anthrax scare.

This page, top: Mick McKnight, me, Anita (became Winn), Mark Robinson, Nick Winn and Andrew Routh going to a fancy dress party in 1979.
Right: Feeding a poorly calf through a stomach tube with milk at Ampleforth College Farm in 1992, assisted by Herd Manager Allen Harrison. I visited the dairy weekly for years – it was one of my favourite jobs.

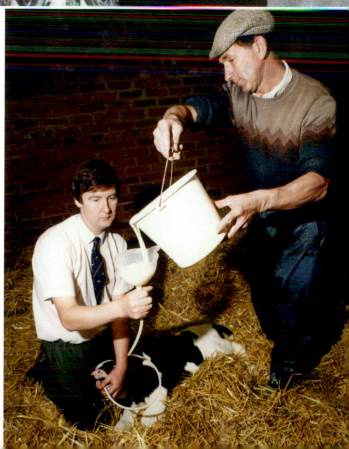

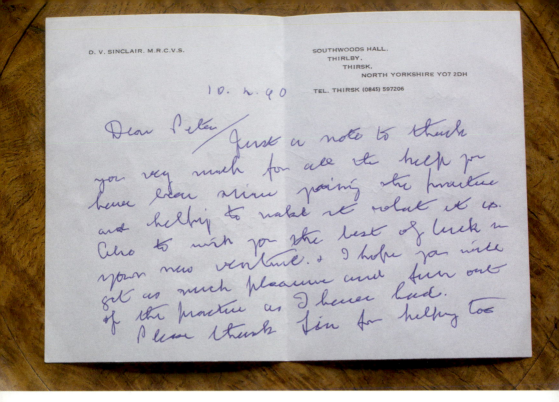

D. V. SINCLAIR. M.R.C.V.S.

SOUTHWOODS HALL.
THIRLBY.
THIRSK.
NORTH YORKSHIRE YO7 2DH
TEL. THIRSK (0845) 597206

10. 4. 90

Dear Peter,

Just a note to thank you very much for all the help you have been since joining the practice and helping to make it what it is. Also to wish you the best of luck in your new venture. & I hope you will get as much pleasure and fun out of the practice as I have had. Please thank Lin for helping too

Above: Letter from Donald Sinclair, on his enforced retirement due to ill health in 1990, thanking me for my efforts to make the practice what it was. **Below:** Me and Lin on our wedding day. L-R, Jim Wight, Gill Wight, me, Lin, Alf Wight, Joan Wight. Front row, Zoe, Katrina and Nicholas Wight. **Opposite:** Always a decent man, Alf kindly loaned me thousands of pounds – and gifted £1000 of it back as a wedding present.

MIRE BECK   THIRLBY THIRSK N. YORKS   YO7 2DJ
TEL. 0845 597360

                              April 3, 1985

Dear Mr Wight,

        I hereby acknowledge that
I have, this day, accepted a loan of
£7,000 (seven thousand pounds), free
of interest, from you, payable on
demand.

Yours sincerely,

P Wright

Peter Wright

Part repayment of £4,000 made on 8-5-86

J A Wright

£1,000 released as wedding present 13-9-86

J A Wright

Final repayment of £2,000 made on 12-11-86

J A Wright

Above: Me on my vintage
Massey Ferguson at Open
Stocking Farm in July 2010.
Right: Here I am with Bertie
the Boxer in 1995. A fantastic
dog with a big personality.
We still miss him.

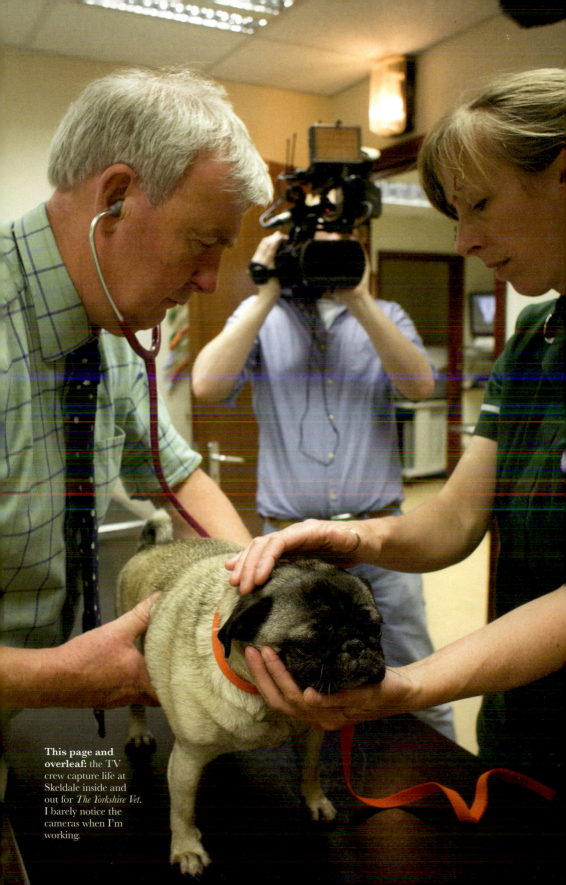

This page and overleaf: the TV crew capture life at Skeldale inside and out for *The Yorkshire Vet*. I barely notice the cameras when I'm working.

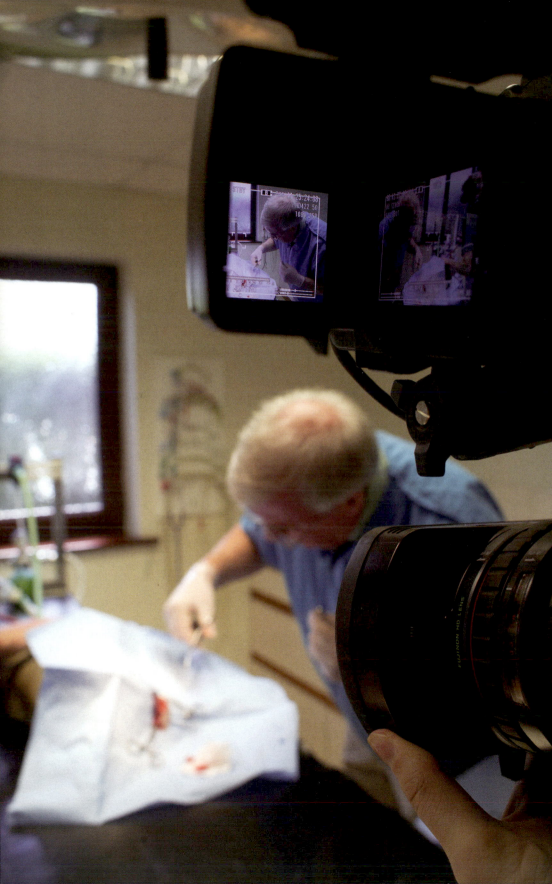

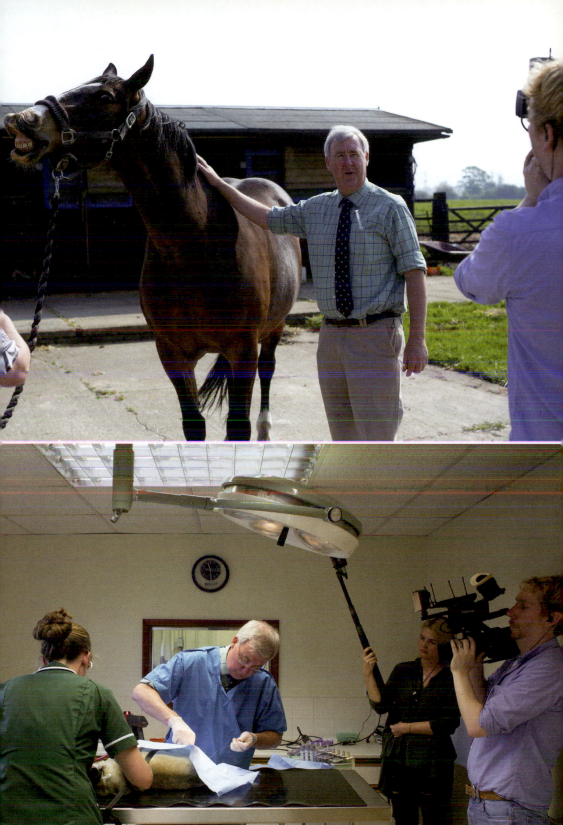

Above: With Heather Corner, my former primary school headmistress at Sessay School, at Sessay's Easter fete in 2017. **Below left:** With my good friends and longstanding farm clients Steve and Jeanie Green and their handful of a cat Storm. **Below right:** I was treating a cow and she coughed at the wrong time… Somewhat worse than egg on your face!

Above: With stars from the original *All Creatures Great and Small* TV series, Christopher Timothy and, below, Robert Hardy. This was the 100 Years of James Herriot celebration on 1st October 2016 at Tennants in Leyburn. Robert stole the show at the party, a mesmerising man even in his final months.

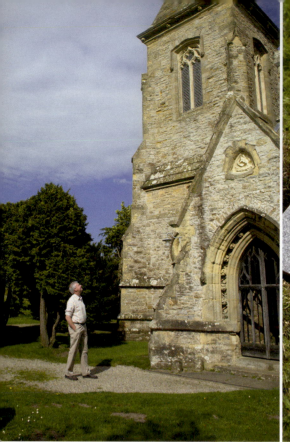

In Loving Memory
FRED DUNCALF
Died 26th January 1973
Aged 72 Years
also his wife
ENA MARY
Died 9th November 2001
Aged 95 Years

Above left: The entrance to Thirkleby Church, where I went to Sunday school as a boy. When my wife Lin was given the news in November 2010 that her cancer had not spread, I went into the church to pray and give thanks.

Above right: My maternal grandparents' headstone in the churchyard at Thirkleby. My Grandad, Fred Duncalf, was the caretaker and church warden for 32 years and Ena, my Granny, used to clean and look after the interior of the church. Fred would light the coke boiler between 11pm and 12am on a Saturday night so the church was warm in winter for the Sunday morning service. **Left:** Me in New York in 2013 after I'd completed a half marathon. It was hard work but great fun. I did it to raise money for cancer charities after Lin was successfully treated for the disease.

Opposite page, top: Me and Lin with our cat Toddy, who was found covered in oil in a skip in 2017. A tiny bundle of fluff then, he's now a full-blown whirlwind of mischief.

Opposite page, bottom: Me and Lin judging the Easter bonnet competition at Sessay village fete in 2017.

The view from the top of Sutton Bank. I sometimes went here with Alf in my younger days to walk his dogs. One of the best views in England! I feel very lucky to live in Yorkshire and be surrounded by such countryside. Who could tire of it? I just hope we can all look after our natural world more, so future generations have the chance to enjoy it too.

over the years by bigger enterprises, but in Joan's heyday they were still a major part of life for her and all the Kirkgate vets.

On my first day of work experience at Kirkgate, Joan remembers me as being "a canny lad" who was a little shy. By the time she left Skeldale in 2003, Alf and Donald (who she always referred to as Mr Wight and Mr Sinclair) had died, Jim had retired and I was one of the bosses, although she never changed the way she addressed me. To her, I was always Peter; she probably never quite shook off the feeling that I was still a schoolboy. My message in Joan's retirement card was heartfelt. "You have seen more changes than me over the lifetime of the practice, but it seems as if the rate of change is speeding up. You were always a constant, stabilising presence, paying attention to details that were vital to the success of the business. When I needed advice, you were always there to provide it."

Joan was there for all of us, including Alf during his Herriot years. She often helped to clear the surgery of his literary fans so we could get on with our real business: treating animals. Alf did reserve some time in the afternoons to sign autographs, though. Some fans were very insistent, and I remember one morning Joan throwing out an American. He must have come back, as later that day Alf told her his name was Nelson Riddle, Frank Sinatra's musical arranger, a man who was probably feted in the US. Alf wasn't at all cross that she'd made him leave – the animals always came first, and he was not a man to be impressed by fame and fortune.

For Joan, Alf was always a boss first and an author second, although she says he was always interested in writing and would often read the short stories in her magazines. She also remembers that around the time his first books were published, she borrowed a library book called *The Hills is Lonely* by Lillian Beckwith. It's about the author's convalescence on an isolated Scottish island, and may have inspired the Herriot content and style; when Joan opened the book she found a piece of paper tucked inside, full of notes in Alf's handwriting. He'd borrowed the book before her and obviously seen a lot to admire.

Meeting Joan now is also a reminder of the changing of the guard at Kirkgate in the late 80s and early 90s, when Alf and Donald both retired, Donald leaving very reluctantly after a stroke. Both men died in 1995. Joan remembers seeing Alf for what turned out to be the last time. He always used to wear heavy waterproof lace-up shoes and had a distinctive walk. When he came into the surgery she'd know it was him without even looking up; but on this particular day she heard someone shuffling along and was startled to see it was Alf, as he'd lost his usual gait.

"I could have cried," she says. "He didn't look too bad, but that shuffle…"

Alf died of cancer a few weeks later, in February. Donald took his own life that June, shortly after the death of his wife Audrey. It was a horrible few months at Kirkgate as we struggled with the loss of the two men who'd not only been the foundation and soul of the practice, but who'd also been our friends and colleagues. It was worse for Jim, though, because Alf was his father. He had to grieve while continuing to work at 23 Kirkgate, a building he'd lived in as a child. It was a very emotional time.

If 1995 was one of the worst periods, there were other episodes that revealed life's ebb as well as its flow. One of these involved police horses again. North Yorkshire Police decided to disband its horse unit and I was asked to help assess and value the animals. It was awful, witnessing the close relationship between the horses and their riders and knowing they soon had to part. When discussing saleable value, many riders came up with a version of this: "It's no good sending him to another force – he's past it and should retire. He's no good in traffic; it spooks him."

What they really meant, of course, was that they wanted to keep their horses. Police horses and riders are a good example of how closely man and beast can work together and the special bond that can develop between them. Some of the horses eventually went to the new Garda Mounted Unit in Ireland, where they no doubt built up good relationships with fresh riders. But in the UK, the decision taken by North Yorkshire Police has been replicated across the country: out of 43 forces, there are now just 12 with police horses.

Another difficult spell was when I contracted brucellosis, something many other vets have had to deal with. It was a reminder that we are sometimes on the front line in the fight against disease. Brucellosis is infectious, with symptoms that include rising and falling fevers, sweats, weakness, headaches and back pain. Some victims develop severe arthritis or depression. Because the disease is transmitted through unpasteurised milk or milk products and direct contact with infected animals and carcasses, vets treating dairy herds used to be particularly at risk, although it has now been eradicated from UK farm stock.

I was in my 30s when I began to suffer from night sweats and flu-like symptoms. After a visit to the doctor and blood tests, brucellosis was the worrying diagnosis. I was put on massive doses of antibiotics for about three months. The GP gave me a magazine so I could read all about the disease, but I threw it away when I got to the section about all the nasty consequences that could arise, such as bone abscesses. Luckily, I recovered.

It was no comfort to discover that Alf had also suffered from brucellosis, but had had it far worse than me. As Jim says in his book about his dad, *The Real James Herriot*: "This disease has been described as a depressive one, but it seemed to have the opposite effect on Alf. He became light-headed and happy lying in bed while cracking jokes to which he, himself, would respond with wild and hysterical laughter."

Brucellosis could have contributed to Alf's mental health problems, which came to a head around 1961. His veterinary friend Eddie Straiton (later an author and broadcaster too) paid for him and Joan to take a holiday in Majorca. They stayed in Eddie's villa, while Eddie himself worked unpaid at Kirkgate for a few weeks until the couple returned, Alf feeling much better.

Eddie thought that brucellosis was probably partly to blame for Alf's prostate cancer, too; the year after his friend's death, he told the author Graham Lord that it might have lowered his resistance. We can't know that for sure, but I am sure of this: Alf would have been concerned, as I was, to find out that a World Health Organisation report in 2006 said brucellosis had been developed experimentally as a biological weapon by state-sponsored programmes. The report said it could be used to attack human and animal populations, and warned the health and veterinary authorities to be aware of it.

Infectious diseases are one thing, but avoidable pain and suffering are something completely different. Julian and I often get letters from *Yorkshire Vet* viewers saying how much they enjoy the programme; some people say they become emotional. I understand that. I've often been overcome myself, pleased when things turn out well and despondent when the outcome is death. But one thing I will never understand is how human beings can deliberately treat animals badly. Unfortunately, it's something I've witnessed many times.

One of the worst things I've seen was when I was a young vet. The RSPCA called me out to a herd of pigs that were being slowly starved to death. They were so hungry they'd begun to eat each other. The owner had horses and dogs, too, and, inexplicably, they were in superb condition. It made the wilful neglect of the pigs even harder to comprehend. I expected the starved animals to be thin and ribby, but was totally unprepared for what I found. Inside the sty were half-eaten bodies of several pigs, with dead piglets lying in the straw and manure. There were sows too weak to stand, utterly emaciated. They'd only survived this long through cannibalism. I felt physically sick. Why didn't the owner just sell the pigs or give them away if he was having difficulty looking after them? Why choose not to feed them? In his 40s, and with no track record of abuse, the man was noncommittal when questioned. He was eventually prosecuted and banned from keeping farm animals. I still ask myself: why would someone do this? And I still have no answer.

Episodes like this continue to crop up. In 2015, a man was arrested after 1,600 pigs were found dead at a farm in Leeds, possibly starved to death. And I was involved in another horrific case of neglect several years ago, when I was asked by the RSPCA to accompany them to a farm near Northallerton. We went to check on three ponies after a tip-off from a horse dealer. It had been raining all day and my spirits were already dampened when we arrived to find an uncooperative farmer in his 60s and his 39-year-old daughter. We called the police even before looking for the animals, as we were worried there might be violence.

Eventually, we found three ponies, two mares aged 12 and a six-year-old stallion, who'd been fed but not cleaned out or allowed outside. They'd been kept for years in a dilapidated outbuilding – the stallion for five years and the mares for two – where their excrement had built up to the extent they were running around on top of it, literally in the rafters. This muck had piled up so high that as we peered through the top half of the door, we could only see their legs, not the top half of their bodies. They had horribly overgrown hooves. The hooves of a horse allowed to roam outdoors wear down, but hooves can grow too long when a horse is kept in a small bedded area. In such cases, a regular trim by a farrier is needed. It's a bit like us going to the barber's every couple of months. The stallion's hooves in particular were so long I remember thinking they resembled skis.

I'd never seen such a mess, and neither had the RSPCA. Inspector Justin Lemasurier said he'd thought this kind of thing had disappeared in the previous century and we both knew there could be associated problems, including irreversible lameness and psychological issues. Before a proper assessment, though, we needed to get the three terrified creatures out of the building, parts of which were on the verge of collapse. The fire brigade was called to help us get inside, as we were worried the building would cave in on us. We then sedated the animals, strapped them onto tarpaulin sheets and, with some difficulty, slid them out. I managed to crudely trim their hooves a little with the help of the firemen and their cutting gear – heavy equipment usually used to free people trapped in cars. The ponies were loaded into a horsebox and taken to the nearest RSPCA equine centre, in County Durham, with me driving behind in case they needed more sedation.

I was keen to monitor their progress and was saddened to hear not long afterwards that the two mares, named Midge and Maisie by RSPCA staff, had to be put to sleep. X-rays had showed their feet were abnormal, the bones within the hooves grossly misshapen. Although Midge was not in as bad a way as Maisie, they were both crippled to some degree by their ordeal, and despite treatment and medication had still been in pain. Even now I'm haunted by the grotesque vision of those poor animals on that horrible day, but I was delighted to learn that the male's hooves – the longest of the three ponies – were gradually trimmed back and he was rehabilitated. He became known as Mungo, and although he suffered from agoraphobia, was completely wild and was frightened of people, he eventually had a full and happy life and was turned out to grass after five months of treatment. To start with he would only venture out when sedated. It took about a year for his hooves to look normal again; he had 31cm, 36cm, 49.5cm, and 50.8cm (12.5in, 14in, 19.5in and 20in) of excess growth removed from his four feet.

Mungo became a companion for showjumping horses and had a particularly close friend called Whiskey, a Shetland pony. They were together for many years until they both passed away in 2017. As for Mungo's owner, the farmer, he was prosecuted, found guilty of causing unnecessary suffering and sentenced to three months in prison. His daughter was put on probation for two years and given 200 hours of community service. The pair were also fined and banned for life from owning animals. Their dastardly deeds and court case featured in the national media, too. In the end, justice was done.

Lin and Peter in their courting days.

CHAPTER 6

A Wheelbarrow for Christmas

It was just before Christmas 1984, and my colleague Tim Yates and I were in the mood for a party. It had been a hectic year and while everyone at Kirkgate had been engrossed in work (Alf's first picture book for children had also just been published) the world outside still encroached. Images of the devastating famine in Ethiopia seemed to be everywhere that December, partly because of Band Aid's 'Do They Know It's Christmas?'. It was all over the airwaves, and even on the playlist at the party that Tim and I organised – the get-together where Lin and I first took serious notice of each other. We'd be married within two years and my life would alter significantly as I adapted to being a husband and, soon after that, a father.

In the days before the Christmas do, I had no idea the evening and its philanthropic musical backdrop would prove to be so pivotal to my future life. Tim and I were mostly focused on organising, deciding where best to have a few bevvies and strut our stuff. I had noticed Lin, the attractive practice manager at the dentist nearby, and had invited her along even though I'd recently bought a property near Thirsk with my girlfriend from university. We didn't see one another much, as she worked a few hours' drive away and neither of us got much time off. Deep down we both knew the relationship was faltering, and I'd asked various family members, friends and colleagues for advice on what to do. Looking back, it's obvious we were limping along, the bungalow and plans to move in together a sticking plaster to cover some gaping holes. I just wish I'd been wise or confident enough to face up to this reality earlier, instead of going through with the purchase.

I pushed the sorry state of my relationship to the back of my mind as Tim and I wondered where to hold our bash. I lived in a house belonging to the practice, but we thought Tim's flat, directly above the operating theatre at Kirkgate, would be a cosier and more atmospheric venue. Now, of course, it's part of the Herriot visitor attraction and full of veterinary paraphernalia, but in 1984 it was a bare and cold bachelor pad. We asked Donald, who owned the building, for his permission, which he immediately gave. As ever, he was keen for his staff to find partners who were not vets, and who were local; the party was an opportunity for that to happen.

Unfortunately, the ceiling of the operating theatre had a massive bow in it and by the next day, Donald had changed his mind, worried we'd bring the whole thing down. A little later, I bumped into Lin and explained our dilemma. She quickly sprang into action, asking her dentist boss if we could use his waiting room instead. He agreed; then Jim's sister Rosie lent us her superior music centre and we stocked up on booze. The party was on.

This evening in our less-than-glamorous location was a roaring success, despite Lin bringing along her suave-looking boyfriend. I hadn't known she had one. He drove a BMW and lived in a nice part of Leeds. Some time later, I took Lin out in my less stylish Ford Escort, which belonged to the practice. She told me afterwards that it stank of pigs and medicines, despite my lashings of aftershave; and I realised that if she was willing to ignore the stench of my car, she must like me.

But that was to come. On the night of the party, we spent most of our time chatting to each other. Her boyfriend wasn't impressed and I felt guilty, but couldn't help myself. Very soon Lin and I managed to untangle ourselves from our other halves and became entangled with each other. During the whirlwind of those early days, I even cooked for her once. Although my beef stroganoff was tasty, I don't think my culinary skills had anything to do with her decision to say "Yes" when I popped the question on Valentine's Day, just a few weeks after that Christmas party.

We soon moved in together, then married in September 1986. Alf and his wife Joan were among the guests on our special day. Part of their gift was a beautiful hand-carved wine table; the other part was a very generous £1,000, which they knocked off the £7,000 interest-free loan they'd given me to buy my ex-girlfriend out of the house we'd bought. Jim and his wife Gill came to the wedding, too, and their daughter Zoe was one of our bridesmaids.

Donald, who liked Lin and was pleased I wasn't marrying a vet, had promised me – twice in writing – that he and Audrey would attend. On the day, though, they were nowhere to be seen. Alf had warned me not to be offended if Donald, a fanatical pigeon fancier, didn't show up. Lin and I were far too busy enjoying our wedding celebrations to hold it against him, and heard that his 50 or so birds were taking part in a major race that day. I knew he loved them. I'd seen him with them at his home, treating them all like the athletes they were, even though he had his favourites. I remember men would come from all over the north of England to the practice with crates full of pigeons, which they would balance on their knees while waiting to see Donald. He was as fascinated by pigeons as he was by horses, and my wedding could never compete with a cross-Channel race.

A couple of years later Tim tied the knot, too. We all took bets as to whether Donald would come, and were amazed when he arrived at the church. We couldn't believe our eyes when he turned up at the reception in Ripon as well. We watched with incredulity, knowing how impatient he was, as he made small talk with guests before the food arrived. However, when we sat down for the meal, we saw two empty spaces where Donald and Audrey should have been. The small talk had been a step too far. Alf told us that it had happened before, when the Sinclairs had been at a big society wedding. The waiter was about to put Donald's dessert down on the table when Audrey politely told him not to bother: her husband had gone fishing.

Lin and I were blessed when our daughter Emily arrived in 1987 and our lives, like those of all new parents, changed overnight. But just as Alf had carried out some TB testing while on his honeymoon in 1941, I too continued to display my commitment to the practice by sometimes working when my family should perhaps have come first. Emily's birth was a case in point. As she was ready to come out, she suddenly moved into a breech position, meaning her feet were poised to emerge first. If Lin had been a cow or a sheep I'd have been able to do something about it, but for once I was helpless. The doctors said Lin needed a caesarean and arranged to admit her to hospital the following afternoon. I obviously wanted to drive her there but, perhaps foolishly, there was something I decided I must do on the way first.

I had always looked after Howard Bosomworth's animals (the farmer with three lambs and a ewe with one teat, mentioned in Chapter 1) and as I've said, continuity with clients is important. He happened to ring the surgery the next morning, saying a couple of his cows had problems. I overheard Joan Snelling tell him I was not available that afternoon and was busy all morning. Another vet could have gone out, of course, but old habits die hard.

"Tell Howard I'll come," I said. "I'm going past there anyway on my way to the hospital."

"Are you sure?" asked Joan, a mother herself – probably wondering what on earth I was doing.

"Yes," I replied. "Lin won't mind."

When I got home I told my apprehensive wife we'd be calling in at Howard's farm on the way to hospital. She didn't say anything, clearly already resigned. We grabbed her overnight bag full of nighties, nappies and baby clothes and set off.

When we pulled into Howard's farmyard he couldn't believe it. "This is no day for a ride out with your wife," he said, as we climbed out of the car and he saw Lin's massive bump.

"Our daughter is about to be born," I said seriously. "I'm taking Lin in for a caesarean."

Howard began to laugh and Lin, clutching her belly, joined in.

"You know what he's like," she said.

While they chuckled away, united in their view of how ridiculous I was, I examined the two cows. I still remember that one had mastitis and the other a cystic ovary. When Lin and I drove away a few minutes later Howard waved us off, his shoulders shaking with laughter. Not long afterwards, I was invited by the consultant obstetrician to watch Lin's caesarean, but declined. I didn't want to see my wife's abdominal contents laid bare. Soon, I was holding our lovely Emily in my arms. I was a father.

Andrew's birth in 1989 went more smoothly, although work impinged there too. With Granny Duncalf, then in her 80s, looking after Emily, Lin and I arrived at the hospital at about 7.30am for a natural birth. As she was not fully dilated I went back to work, spending a couple of hours checking that the facilities were up to scratch at the local turkey factory. I was back at Lin's side by about 2pm, but she was still far from ready to push.

There happened to be a test match on between Australia and England, so I kept disappearing to the visitors' room to watch TV before nipping back to see Lin. She even came to watch the cricket for a bit, although she's no fan of the sport. I like to think it helped to distract her from her pain for a few minutes. Andrew finally arrived a few hours later on what had been a gruelling but happy day for Lin. It was happy for me too – despite Australia's victory.

I'm not the only Yorkshireman to have behaved a little insensitively when their children are born. For a few decades I've known a delightful, gentle farmer who used to milk about 60 cows and deliver their mouthwatering yield around his village. Let's call him Bill. One day, when I was chatting to his wife about Christmas, she asked me what I'd bought for Lin.

At that point our children were small and we were building a new house. I told her we didn't have much spare cash for presents, before asking her what she might be getting from Bill. "Is he not the sort of man to leap off a cliff into the sea with a box of chocolates, like in the TV advert?" I said.

"You must be joking," she giggled. "Last Christmas he bought me a new wheelbarrow so I could move our newborn calves from where they'd been born into the calf house."

Then she told me that years earlier, while she'd been recovering in hospital after giving birth, Bill had turned up clutching a bunch of flowers.

"I was overcome," said his wife. "In all our years courting he'd never bought me flowers. Tears welled up in my eyes. I glanced up at him and said, 'Oh Bill. They're lovely.' Then he put them down on the bed and said, 'Mr Braithwaite sent you them.'"

When she'd finished the story we both burst out laughing. I still see "Bill" sometimes, leaning on his wall looking for someone to chat to. He's a retired widower now; his daughter does a milk round and his grandson keeps a few cows. I don't know if he ever got round to buying his wife a romantic present, but I got the impression she really wasn't bothered.

I had a new family and they obviously took priority, but my colleagues were becoming increasingly important to me as well. I've talked about Alf, Donald and Jim, and *Yorkshire Vet* viewers have often seen me with my former partner Julian, whom I've known for more than 20 years. But I've not said much yet about Skeldale vet Tim, who was also at Kirkgate. He joined us in 1984, not long before that special Christmas party. He's now as close as family and we've shared many experiences, including the night of my stag do. Jim kept off the booze and was our designated taxi driver, but Tim, usually a quiet and dignified fellow, took the opportunity to put away more than a few. The following day I was suffering from an almighty hangover – and a punctured eardrum, damaged by the privet hedge I'd been pushed into for a joke while I was answering the call of nature. Nursing a throbbing ear and a pounding headache, and having been told off by Lin, who feared my injury might prevent us from flying to America for our honeymoon, I went to the practice to collect some medication for a friend's dog. I found Tim standing in the operating theatre, not a patient in sight. On his face was an oxygen mask. "Oxygen… good for hangovers?" he mumbled, breathing in deeply. Luckily, neither of us was on duty that day.

About 30 years later I found myself working alongside Tim in a torrential downpour one Boxing Day. We'd been called out by a farmer with pedigree Aberdeen Anguses – beautiful prize-winning animals that produced fantastic meat. On this particular day we were needed for a caesarean, which we often do in pairs at Skeldale, just as we did at Kirkgate. It's useful to have another pair of sterile hands to hold the uterus. It's also a good opportunity to teach the younger vets. This time it happened to be Tim and me on call. We left our families to their turkey sandwiches, trifle and petty squabbling and set off, only to find some of the roads flooded. Tim had to go a long way round in his car, which wasn't suited to deep water. I had a 4x4 but was still struggling, and passed a number of vehicles that had been abandoned in floodwater. As we sometimes say in Yorkshire, it was raining so hard it was coming down like stair rods.

Eventually, we arrived to see that the portable crush to restrain the pregnant cow had been set up, which was good news. The noisy patient was already inside: more good news. The bad news was, the crush was outside in the pouring rain. Tim and I got out our kit and put it on some bales, off the sodden and muddy ground. We put on our green sterile tops, our bare arms sticking out from the short sleeves. Someone – the cow, the calf, Tim or me – is going to get pneumonia, I remember thinking. Without having to talk, because we work together so well, the calf was pulled out as the rain hammered down relentlessly. It might not have been baby Jesus on Christmas Day, but a newborn Angus on Boxing Day was not a bad sight. As we closed up the mother it was still raining and we were soaked, but smiling nevertheless. We looked like two drowned rats as we drove away, our underwear squelching on our car seats. Luckily, neither of us took ill. The cow and her calf never looked back either.

Tim and I have now moved up the ranks to become grey-haired business partners, but our friendship has remained constant, based as it is on mutual respect and affection. We've never had an argument and have never lost our love of curing animals. As Donald used to say, a veterinary partnership is like a marriage: easy to get into, but not easy to get out of. He was sometimes an awkward man who could make Alf's life difficult, and was reluctant to allow new partners to join the practice, including Jim and me. But Tim and I have never had any issues and have always made decisions by consensus. Long may our successful "marriage" continue.

It was clear that Tim and I would get on from the very beginning, but some things are not always so obvious. I've hopefully grown wise enough to realise that appearances can be deceptive, a lesson I first started to learn while still at Luton when I came across Dobermann dogs for the first time. They are renowned for being aggressive and untrustworthy, partly because they were often used as guard dogs in German concentration camps in the second world war. It was 1982 and I was still wet behind the ears, so when I looked at the appointment book for the next day and saw I was down to see two Dobermanns called Killer and Mauler, I was more than slightly apprehensive. I quickly looked up their records, but got no clue as to their temperaments; but I did notice that the dogs were young, making it even easier for them to rip my throat out.

I had a sleepless night and was dreading going to work. After an uneventful morning seeing a few cats and dogs, I went to the waiting room door with a massive pit in my stomach. The two Dobermanns were there on leads held by their smiling owner. I froze slightly, then beckoned them, imagining one of the animals breaking free and jumping on my back, my head in its jaws.

I strode swiftly into the consulting room where the man picked up one dog and put it on the table.

"This is Mauler," he said.

"Does he live up to his name?" I stuttered.

"Not at all," he laughed.

I tentatively reached out and patted the dog, and was surprised when he began licking my hand. As I stroked his face I could see from his eyes that he was a kind, gentle chap. Killer was just as sweet, rolling over to show me his belly. What a relief!

Like all vets, I'm still sometimes wary of a few dogs. While I've found some Rottweilers to be absolutely lovely, a few have been unpredictable. The Greens – whose lovely farm I've already mentioned – once gave me a birthday cake with the face of a Rottweiler on the top because they couldn't find one that resembled my boxer. They weren't to know I've been attacked on more than one occasion by a Rottweiler; it's the thought that counts, and I enjoyed my gift, particularly when there were only a few crumbs left of the Rottweiler's face staring back at me. But since that first encounter in Luton I've been a big Dobermann fan, and have seen hundreds of them over the last 35 years. They are intelligent, friendly and energetic. Killer and Mauler? More like Pacifist and Softie.

I've had many encounters with potentially dangerous dogs, but some episodes stick in my mind more than others. Lin and I have some friends who used to live in a village not far from us. They had horses and a livery yard with two German Shepherd guard dogs. One was said to be even-tempered, but even our friends were wary of the other. When I was asked to go and check his ear I agreed, but only if he wore a muzzle. I knew the dog would attack if I was in his territory, so I wanted that clever bit of leather keeping his teeth from my flesh.

Not long afterwards I went back to the yard with Lin and my mother-in-law Ann on a social call. Ann is an animal fan too, but unlike me she's had several German Shepherds and won't hear a word said against them. When we arrived we got out of the car and began walking into the horses' yard in the mistaken belief the two dogs were safely locked up. Suddenly, I saw them – not only out and about, but staring directly at us.

We've had it, I thought, then began yelling at Ann, who was several steps in front of me. Unfortunately she's quite deaf, and didn't respond to my frantic calls; even if she'd heard, I would have been wasting my breath.

"Ooooh, German Shepherds," she said, making a beeline for the dogs. They stood dead still while she walked up to them, without fear or seemingly a care in the world. "Helllloooooo," she said.

Then they all began playing together as if they were long-lost mates.

I couldn't believe my eyes. "Ann, that one's a killer!" I shouted.

"Isn't he luuurvely," she chortled.

Our friend, the owner, was horrified – and, it's fair to say, as gobsmacked as I was. Studies have shown that people who are anxious around dogs are more likely to get bitten. I'm not sure how true that is, but it would certainly explain why my mother-in-law was able to wade in as she did and come to no harm.

Perhaps surprisingly, our feline friends can sometimes be pretty nasty too. *Yorkshire Vet* viewers might have seen me trying to deal with Possum, a particularly vicious cat. I need a pair of leather gauntlets to protect me from her wrath when I try to treat her. Sometimes, with other cats, I use towels or blankets; Alf was a dab hand at wrapping up hissing and scratching felines, a skill he passed on to me.

At the other end of the size scale are other potentially lethal animals. Many people have been maimed or killed by intimidating bulls, including some farmers I know. I've often stepped out of the way in the nick of time as a young bull has come at me. I heard the tragic story not long ago of a vet being gored by a bull and paralysed. It could have been me, or Jim, or any of us. Our profession, for all the light-heartedness of the Herriot books and *The Yorkshire Vet*, can be dangerous, and I've often been proved right in my initial assessment of a situation or animal.

I had a really nasty scare one winter morning recently when I was attacked by a Central Asian shepherd dog. It was the closest I've come to "death by dog". These animals are sometimes called *volkodav*, which means "wolf crusher" in Russian. Vet-killer would also be appropriate, if you ask me. The man I was visiting had a dog and a bitch to deter prowlers at his property. The bitch had been suffering from a vaginal polyp and I'd already performed a hysterectomy at the surgery. As her stitches were due out, I told the owner I'd call in to remove them. He'd already told me the male dog was a killer who he would not trust with anyone outside the family, but said the female was calmer.

As I got out of my car I had misgivings, but felt reasonably sure the owner would have his animals under control. He brought the bitch out of her secure shed and held her as I examined her healing wound and stitches. Suddenly, I felt my arm gripped as if in the jaws of a vice. The male dog had sneaked out. He had not barked or growled, but had simply flown at me. I had a coat on but he tore through that and through my jumper and shirt as he moved like lightning, working his way up my body. For a few seconds I thought my time was up. Standing on their back legs, these dogs are about 2 metres (7ft) tall and this one was almost at my neck when the owner managed to wrestle him off me.

I was lucky to be wearing a coat and lucky it was a thick one. I can't bear to think what could have happened if I'd been a child, or if the animal had actually got to my throat. I was very shaken and quickly left. Later, the owner rang me to apologise, perhaps worried I would sue him. I told him I wouldn't, as I'd never sued anyone and didn't intend to start then; but I did expect a new coat. I also told him he would be held responsible if the dog ever killed anyone.

I don't know whether my words made him properly consider the consequences and responsibilities of owning such a dangerous dog, but it was a reminder that ethical and moral dilemmas frequently pop up when you least expect them. In *The Yorkshire Vet*, the soft and sentimental side of the job is the one that's mostly portrayed, but there is a darker side. I think I mostly come across as rather jolly on screen, but regular viewers have probably heard me say I'm naturally a glass half-empty man. I was told in my early years to downplay the chances of any treatment's success. My bosses, particularly Alf, thought it best if clients believed there was little hope. He would regularly say, "Always paint a black picture." We'd be heroes if things went well, he reasoned, while our failures would be more readily accepted if circumstances conspired against us.

This was never truer than when I was tasked with the only pig hysterectomy I've ever done – a job I undertook at the very beginning of my career, in Luton. I went out to see a sow, a new mother with a prolapsed uterus (farmers would say she'd "put her pig bed out"). When I arrived, she was lying down looking pathetic and uncomfortable, her ten piglets still suckling at her teats. Her uterus was hanging outside her body and she'd managed to trample on it. It looked like raw liver; some of the tissue was dirty and torn. She could easily have died there and then of shock. On any regular day I'd have arranged for her to be slaughtered on the farm and sent to a butcher quickly, so she'd still qualify as meat for human consumption. But this was a bank holiday and no abattoir or butcher was open. I couldn't send the animal to hospital: I was both the doctor and the hospital. It was all down to me. There was no way I could get the uterus back inside the poor creature, but in the recesses of my mind I remembered that there was another possible option: a hysterectomy, even though I'd been taught at university that it was considered a waste of time because the sow would invariably die of shock. I told the farmer we could put her to sleep or we could try the operation, explaining carefully it was a very difficult procedure and almost certain to fail. But this was a holiday, as I've said, and the farmer would get no money for the sow if she died. Plus, I could tell he was a compassionate man; he wanted me to give her a chance.

This is going to be terrible, I thought. She couldn't possibly survive. But I tried to ignore the devil on my shoulder, appearing far more confident than I felt. Surprisingly, the pig was still alive after I'd operated. She'll definitely be dead by morning, I told myself with conviction. I left, putting the image of the sow out of my mind; so it was a pleasant surprise when four days later the delighted farmer telephoned me to say his pig was alive and doing well. She went on to rear all her piglets. I felt 10 feet tall, even though I'd got lucky in an operation in which I had nothing much to lose. I've enjoyed telling the tale to my veterinary friends and colleagues, most of whom have never even tried to perform a pig hysterectomy.

Nowadays, there's a lot of concern in the profession about being sued, but in the 1980s it was far less common, so we'd be more likely to roll up our sleeves and try something even when the odds were stacked against us. That pig hysterectomy taught me that it's good practice to be pessimistic, because it can smooth the relationship between and vet and client. Mostly, though, I learnt that there are occasions when it feels marvellous to be proved completely wrong.

Farmers and vets are sometimes seen as callous because they care for animals, like the pig with the prolapsed uterus, only for them to be eventually killed and eaten. How can we stand getting to know a pig or cow, the argument goes, then munch on a bacon sandwich or a burger? It does seem like a paradox, one I've encountered countless times. I saw many farming friends reduced to tears during the foot-and-mouth crisis, when their herds were routinely slaughtered by the government (even if they weren't sick) in an attempt to contain the disease. Their anguish wasn't because of economics: all of them received compensation for their lost stock. They cried because they loved their animals. Richard, a butcher I know, kills animals for a living; his job means meat-eaters don't have to do the slaughtering themselves. But he and his partner Sybil are very committed to animal welfare. Recently, I witnessed the couple's anguish when a moorhen they regularly saw was knocked down and killed on a road near my house by a speeding car.

I myself have been asked several times how I can justify saving lives for a job and then go home and eat meat. I'm seen on the television looking after farm animals as well as pets, often talking to them and patting them while I try to keep them alive and well for as long as possible. I can see how some people might find my efforts to save a lamb, say, and my own desire to eat roast lamb difficult to square in their minds. Part of this is tradition. I grew up on a farm, where I'd see animals disappear and then turn up on the dinner table. That was the world I knew, and the one I still live in. I have a job to do, and am paid by farmers to treat their livestock. I also enjoy eating meat as part of a balanced diet and feel we have a right to do so. However, that doesn't mean I think we should treat animals cruelly. While they are alive, they should be kept in the best conditions possible, and slaughtered humanely. When I eat meat I buy it from local producers so I know where the animal has come from and am aware of the conditions it's been reared in.

If a farmer, or anyone else connected with the food industry, falls short of these high standards, I am completely in favour of them being prosecuted. The actions of four men at Bowood – a halal abattoir near Thirsk – who were filmed with hidden cameras treating animals with horrific cruelty, were disgraceful, but thankfully not the norm. In early 2018 they were sentenced, after some harrowing details emerged in court. Their punishments – including suspended prison sentences and hundreds of hours of unpaid community work – were welcome but, I thought, didn't go far enough. The government's Food Standards Agency hoped the sentences sent "a clear message to other abattoirs that fail to uphold the required standards: we will investigate and we will look to prosecute".

Selina Scott, the former television presenter from Scarborough, is interested in animal welfare; among other things, she campaigns to ban the export of live animals. However, in my opinion she was wrong to dive into the uproar over the abattoir the way she did, going public with her criticism of Thirsk in a letter to the *Times*. She accused the town of hypocrisy for promoting its association with James Herriot while the abattoir was operating in its midst. She was totally wrong to imply we didn't care, as staff from the Herriot museum and other local residents were actually among about 50 people who held a protest when the mistreatment of the animals at the abattoir was first revealed. One woman even shouted: "What would James Herriot think of this?" As Jim said in his own letter to the *Times* about Ms Scott's outburst, "The maintenance of high welfare standards in abattoirs is the responsibility of vets employed by the Food Standards Agency, and has nothing to do with the people of Thirsk or the local veterinary practices."

We can't control what goes on behind closed doors; we can only spring into action when lights are shone in dark places. Although what happened at Bowood was illegal, there are sometimes issues in life that are legally acceptable but morally wrong – such as, indeed, the export of live animals. What we can all try to do is attempt to influence our families, friends and communities, and hopefully our politicians, through our actions and words. Knowing the provenance of our food and ensuring every meat supplier adheres to the best welfare and hygiene standards – imports too – is a good place to start, if we want to eat well and treat animals with compassion and respect. Choosing our food carefully and understanding how it's produced or grown can help to change the world for the better.

The church and school at Sessay, which Peter attended as a child.

CHAPTER 7

An Evening with Sir David Attenborough

As a child, I often went with my Granny and Grandad Duncalf to the local church. Grandad was a church warden; Granny helped to tidy up. I would play while they worked. It's not surprising, then, that I know so many hymns, including many people's favourite, "All Things Bright and Beautiful". The song's second line, "All creatures great and small", is familiar to almost everyone in the UK, religious or not. It became the title of one of the Herriot books and also the name of the hit BBC TV series.

I would never have imagined, singing that hymn as a boy, that this line and the world of television would come to have such significance for me. These days, filming for *The Yorkshire Vet* has made my hectic life even busier. I've had to get used to cameras watching me; by and large, I've adjusted well. But although I've had a few years on TV now, there are still times when I'm unsure how to act and can easily come unstuck.

One such occasion was in January 2018, when Julian and I attended the National Television Awards at the O2 arena with Paul Stead and Lou Cowmeadow from Daisybeck Studios, our programme's production company. After an uneventful journey to the capital, the congestion across London was horrendous so by the time we made it to the 453-room Intercontinental Hotel, we'd missed lunch. Around 4pm, we changed into our glad rags, complete with black ties. I was hoping for something to eat before setting off for the event, but there wasn't time. Paul said there would be nibbles at the do.

No one seemed interested in Julian and me on the red carpet going in. And why would they be? We're two scruffy country vets from Thirsk who've been thrust into the world of TV, which can be a strange beast. We were told that there would be a car to take us the short distance from our hotel to the O2 arena: we could have easily walked, but apparently had to arrive in style. I felt like a rabbit caught in the headlights as the paparazzi clicked away at Tony Audenshaw, the Emmerdale actor, just ahead of us. Paul, Daisybeck's boss, kept telling Julian and me to slow down and make the most of the moment. But people were not looking for the Yorkshire Vets; they wanted to see big names, such as the actress Julie Walters and naturalist and international icon Sir David Attenborough. The photographers wanted the stars to preen and pose. For real celebrities, the red carpet provides an opportunity to show off; I was just terrified, and relieved when we got inside. I quickly found myself chatting to Tony Audenshaw, who seemed very down to earth. When he said his in-laws were farmers I immediately relaxed, and we talked about how lucky we were to live in beautiful places.

Although I enjoyed my moment in the celebrity spotlight, I still cringe a little when I think about that night; my actions and words weren't helped by a mostly empty stomach, into which a few glasses of red wine were poured, although I did ignore the champagne because it always gives me indigestion. Before we sat down, Paul introduced me to a glamorous woman called Ruth Langsford and I asked her what she did. Paul almost choked on his wine. If Lin had been there to help me, I'd have known Ruth was a well-known TV presenter, married to Eamonn Holmes (whom I had heard of). I'd known I wouldn't be able to recognise everyone; Lin had even texted Paul beforehand to say I wasn't good at picking out celebrities, and asked him to help me. As Ruth walked away I wanted the ground to swallow me up. But then I told myself that while she's on TV, I'm usually busy calving cows or seeing itchy dogs and sneezing cats. It's no wonder I don't know every star.

The Yorkshire Vet had not been nominated for an award, but we still sat among the nominees, not far from the stage and just behind the *Emmerdale* contingent. After watching the awards for a while I needed the men's room. I'd just emerged into the corridor when I spotted Mark Labbett, the so-called "Beast" from the ITV quiz show *The Chase*. I love the programme, and as the alcohol was now kicking in I started to feel less shy. I marched over to introduce myself, and asked him to take a selfie with me. It was a lovely little interlude with one of my heroes and I cherish the photo, even if there's not much of me in it – Mark is a big man.

There was a massive cheer when *Eastenders'* nomination for Best Serial Drama was announced, which wasn't surprising given that we were in London. The cheer for Yorkshire's *Emmerdale* was rather muted in comparison, and I felt as if I was supporting the away team at a football match. Julie Walters then announced the winner: *Emmerdale*. I was definitely tipsy by that point, as I'd only eaten some tiny canapes – a fancy word for nibbles. I leapt to my feet and applauded – unfortunately, a second or two before anyone else, so I ended up standing there on my own shouting and cheering. Lin, watching on TV at home, texted me a few minutes later to say she'd had a good laugh. At least it was another accolade for my beloved Yorkshire.

The highlight of the night was watching Sir David Attenborough accept an award for the *Blue Planet II* documentary series. He's a hero to so many people, including former US president Barack Obama, and has, for years, been connected to Britain's Wildlife Trusts. These include the legendary Yorkshire Wildlife Trust (YWT) which was only the second wildlife or naturalists' trust established in Britain, and of which Jim and I are both proud members.

"People nationwide look to the Yorkshire Trust for leadership," Sir David said in York in 2016, when the YWT celebrated its 70th birthday. "Politicians now actually care about what you say, and the more vociferous you are, the more they will take notice."

You can't help but admire his dedication as he highlights what we're doing to our natural environment, including our addiction to plastic. When Sir David talks, people listen: you could have heard a pin drop in the arena that night. He said: "What we were all trying to do is to raise an issue, which is of great importance. Not only to this country, but worldwide." He added that if his team's television programmes helped to stir consciences "and we are going to do something to protect our beautiful world, then all of us will be very pleased."

After the ceremony, everyone went to the bar. By this time I was moving effortlessly around the room, although I was being followed closely by Paul, who was by now watching my every move. The next day I chuckled to myself; the awards ceremony reminded me of a Herriot story about the young vet going to a party at a client's very posh home. Mrs Pumphrey, one of the most popular characters in the books, owned an obese Pekingese called Tricki Woo. The dog's vet, his "Uncle Herriot", was invited to a wonderful evening of drinks and dancing in a ballroom complete with chandeliers and a five-piece orchestra. James drinks copious amounts of champagne served by white-jacketed waiters and then dances the night away with several ladies, young and old. He thinks his conversation becomes increasingly witty as the evening wears on – and the same feeling crossed my mind in London. As Herriot put it so well, "I caught sight of myself in a mirror: a distinguished figure, glass in hand, the hired suit hanging on me with quiet grace. It took my breath away." Or was that just the drink talking?

Later on that evening, when I spotted the comedian and presenter Paul O'Grady, who'd just won a special recognition award for his TV series *For the Love of Dogs*, I was feeling confident enough to approach him. I might have even walked more or less in a straight line. I remember saying I admired him for highlighting the plight of homeless dogs, and invited him up to Thirsk. I do hope he will visit one day. We have a spare room waiting and countless dog stories to discuss.

Just after I'd moved away from him, I felt a shove, and someone drunk bumped into me and tipped red wine over my white shirt. I zigzagged to the men's room and splashed handfuls of water down my front, returning to the party sopping wet. Luckily, it was fairly dark so I don't think anyone noticed, and by that point I wouldn't have cared if they had. James Herriot, well and truly drunk, was called out to deliver several piglets after the party at Mrs Pumphrey's, but I got off lightly at the TV awards. All I had to do was deliver myself to bed.

There have been many other memorable occasions that have resulted from my involvement with *The Yorkshire Vet*, including getting to know the Welcome to Yorkshire tourism boss Gary Verity. He's a legend in my eyes, promoting Yorkshire and leading the successful campaign to get the start of the 2014 Tour de France held in God's Own Country. It's also been fun meeting people like cricketer Geoffrey Boycott and comedians Cannon and Ball; Lin and I took Tommy Cannon around the Herriot museum. On one occasion, Julian and I headlined an event called Countryside Live in front of thousands of people in Harrogate; I can't quite believe I overcame my shyness to do it. Then recently, I was proud to receive an honorary degree from Harper Adams University in Shropshire for making a significant contribution to raising the profile of the veterinary profession.

On a lighter note, I've even taken part in a fashion show and turned on Christmas lights. I've presented awards and enjoyed being in another Daisybeck production for Channel 5, *Springtime on the Farm*. This programme explored a joyful but busy time, with much of the filming taking place in a barn full of noisy goats, sheep and donkeys at Cannon Hall Farm near Barnsley, run by Roger Nicholson and his sons. I took part in three episodes during the chilly spring of 2018, and although it wasn't live TV it was still quite nerve-racking. Farmer and BBC *Countryfile* frontman Adam Henson and Lindsey Chapman, from BBC2's *Springwatch Unsprung*, were the very polished presenters. It was fascinating to see them and the rest of the 20 or so crew hard at work. Presenter Gloria Hunniford also took part, as did former *Emmerdale* actor Kelvin Fletcher (Andy

Sugden) and JB Gill, who used to be in the boy band JLS. I'd never heard of JLS until I arrived at the farm, but I know all about them now. He seemed a nice lad and was featured on the programme because he presents a TV series about farming for children. He has several acres in Kent and keeps pigs and turkeys.

Working in television for the last few years has given me an insight into a world I previously knew nothing about. At Cannon Hall Farm there was a makeup woman to paint and powder our faces in the Green Room, where performers and presenters can relax before the action gets underway. It was there that I studied pre-filmed segments for the show, chatted to the crew and other guests, and tucked into a huge plate of lasagne and chips. Frustratingly, the planned script got altered so I was sometimes asked questions I hadn't prepared for, which kept me on my toes. In one episode, the Greens took part and were treated as farming royalty. Jeanie was selfless, as usual. She and Steve had both been given blankets and hot-water bottles while they waited in the wings, but she immediately passed hers to her husband, who's several years older than her. She made everyone laugh, as she always does.

My fun few days at Cannon Hall ended with a "wrap party" in the farm's bar. I couldn't drink as I was driving back to Thirsk, and also had to be up for work the next day. Paul from Daisybeck stood on a chair and gave a speech while the glasses clinked, thanking everyone involved. Later, while Lin and I were getting ready for bed, she called out to me from the bathroom.

"Peter, don't forget to take your makeup off!" she said, before bursting out laughing: another reminder of the bizarre world of TV I'd found myself in.

Springtime on the Farm was certainly a nice break from my usual routine, but I was relieved when the filming was over and I could get back to everyday life. I ask myself sometimes how I got into all this, as I still think of myself as a country bumpkin. Previously, I would say no to requests for filming; Skeldale was approached many years before the first series of *The Yorkshire Vet* to do a documentary, looking at how the veterinary world had changed since the Herriot days. We refused, wary of our work being interrupted; we wanted to concentrate on building up the pet side of the business, knowing that small farms were fading away and we were losing many of those clients. We'd also seen how much the media had demanded of Alf's time, and how he'd been catapulted, somewhat unwillingly, into the spotlight. Sometimes he'd been almost forced into performing for the cameras – for example, he might be asked to run around catching a pig. He often felt uncomfortable in these situations. After Jim retired in 2000, leaving Tim, Julian and me in charge, I felt the pressure to protect Alf and Donald's legacy even more. Donald often welcomed change, but he was also very erratic, sometimes saying, "Don't rock my boat." I was adamant that we should not do anything that he or Alf might not have approved of, even though they were no longer around.

It was in late 2014 that I opened an email from Daisybeck Studios in Leeds, which said they'd been commissioned by Channel 5 to film a veterinary practice that dealt with both pets and farm animals, and that embraced the original Herriot ethos and values. They knew our Herriot pedigree and asked for a chat. I mentioned the note to Tim and Julian, but was too busy to think much about it. A few weeks went by and another email arrived, requesting a meeting. I must have been a little intrigued, as I said yes, but didn't think it would lead anywhere. I felt Herriot, vets and animals had been well covered; there was nothing left to say. I also didn't want the Herriot legacy to be tainted by something tacky and tawdry.

After an initial meeting, I still didn't want Skeldale to be involved. Julian was interested, but Tim wasn't at all. He is one of the best and most dependable vets I've ever met, but has always shunned the limelight. Later, I found out Daisybeck was now saying, "Skeldale, Skeldale, Skeldale. It has to be Skeldale." They'd talked to around 50 other practices, but had their sights set firmly on us. I still said no, even when Paul explained he wanted to show our friendliness, our strong bond with clients and the fact we deal with all creatures great and small, unlike other practices that only treat pets or focus on farm animals or horses.

Fortunately, Daisybeck didn't give up; gradually, their persistence began to pay off. I lay in bed at night chewing it all over. We could fail with this, I thought, but then again we might not. I began to think that if Skeldale didn't agree, we would regret it; but when Paul rang me just before Easter 2015 asking for my decision, I still couldn't say what it was. He had deadlines to meet and a crew lined up, and said he had a second choice sorted out if I said no. That took the pressure off, but I didn't want to leave him floundering. I agreed I'd make a decision over Easter.

By now Julian was all for it, but in my mind I was still to-ing and fro-ing. On the Tuesday afternoon I picked the phone up and called Paul, not even knowing what I was going to say.

"Now then 'vitnry' (a Yorkshireism for veterinary), have you made a decision?" he said.

"I've given it a lot of thought, Paul, and have decided we'll give it a go."

My words surprised him; he told me later he'd been expecting a no. I surprised myself too, but before I could change my mind he said he wanted filming to start the very next day. If I didn't like how the first day went, I could stop the whole project.

"I don't think it will be a success," I told him. "You're ploughing all this money into it and it's all been done before. But we'll give it a try."

A key reason I finally agreed to do the programme was that I had come to trust Paul. He's creative, a former radio and TV presenter in his 50s who plays the piano, whereas I have a more scientific mind. In many ways we are opposites, but somehow we seem to complement each other. I grew up on a farm and Paul grew up on a council estate in Wakefield. I didn't know him well at all, but I believe in trusting people, and I had come to feel that he wouldn't let me, the practice or Herriot's legacy down.

The first cameraperson to arrive at Skeldale was Izzy. She was brilliant, and discreet, with a good sense of humour. When we were working, we hardly knew she was filming, and she was very professional with our clients. We felt as if we'd known her for years. Julian and I agreed the initial filming had gone well, and Tim said he had no problem with us going ahead, as long as he was not involved. I told Paul we were on. Soon, other Daisybeck crew were regularly appearing at Skeldale, including Lou Cowmeadow, appropriately named for someone working on an animal programme; she's now the series editor. One of her many tasks was arranging for the actor Christopher Timothy, who played James Herriot in the TV series, to do the voiceover. I was a little wooden early on, and found some of the filming and questions a little strange as I went about my work. But Ian Ashton, the boss of the Herriot museum, always reminded me that the programme would be good for Thirsk and Yorkshire, and after a while I got used to having a camera crew following me around everywhere. I must admit, I now quite enjoy it.

In the autumn of 2015, just before the first series of *The Yorkshire Vet* went out on Channel 5, Thirsk's Ritz cinema had a premiere of the first episode. We even had a red carpet that Paul had found on eBay for £200. There were about 100 people in the musty old building where Alf had taken his future wife Joan on one of their first dates. Now here Julian and I were, about to be on national TV. Were we also about to wreck the Herriot legacy, the caring ethos that prevailed at Kirkgate, then at Skeldale? I hope I hid my fears when Julian and I gave our speeches. I think I even managed to smile and talk coherently, overcoming my usual shyness, although I was fighting grief: my father had died a few weeks before, following a short illness. He would have enjoyed every minute of *The Yorkshire Vet*. My mother couldn't attend the premiere either, because of her disappearance into the abyss that is Alzheimer's. My brother took her a *Yorkshire Vet* mug. She was often confused (she died in June 2018), but when she saw the photo of my face on it she immediately said, "That's my son, Peter." When I visited soon afterwards, though, she stared at me and said, "Just remind me again who you are?"

So the excitement and fun of making the programme came at a time of great personal sadness, but that's often the way of things – the highs and lows arriving together. Seeing this first instalment on the big screen, I realised Daisybeck Studios had captured the very essence of Skeldale and our Yorkshire countryside. It took my breath away.

When Episode One was broadcast on television, I was out playing bridge, as always on a Tuesday. My routine and my life began to alter from that first night; when I got home, Lin read me some of the enthusiastic reactions to *The Yorkshire Vet* on social media. I began to sleep more easily when I realised the programme had quickly become a hit with the public. The first few series attracted more than a million viewers, with over 2 million watching Series 4. We filmed Series 7 in early 2018. Jim and his sister Rosie are fans; she sometimes telephones after an episode to say how much she liked it. It's a relief to know it's going down well with the Wight family.

I now meet *Yorkshire Vet* fans all over the place; I've bumped into Australians in Thirsk who watch the programme Down Under, and I've even been asked for my autograph at the Taj Mahal in India. However, I'd like to think my newfound fame hasn't gone to my head. Lin never fails to remind me that people watch *The Yorkshire Vet* primarily for the animals, not the vet, who's usually covered in muck. Just before I was due to give a speech in a church a few months ago, a friend leaned across the pew and gave me a tissue, whispering to me to wipe the corner of my right eye. I still had a tiny bit of cow dung on my face, despite two showers, having been completely covered that day while treating an uncooperative patient.

Something I really love about *The Yorkshire Vet* is knowing children enjoy it. It's thrilling to meet them, read their letters and think I'm helping to get a few of them off their Xboxes, and inspiring another generation to take more of an interest in animals. As predicted, thousands more people, including lots of youngsters, are now visiting the Herriot museum thanks to the programme. I'm also very aware that I can use my so-called "celebrity" as a force for good. For example, I've been part of a Channel 5 campaign to celebrate the magic of home and what home means. The campaign highlights the awful problem of homelessness, working with homelessness charity Crisis and many famous faces (far better known than me), including singer Jane McDonald and *Blackadder* actor, comedian and presenter Tony Robinson.

I also support a charity called Street Paws, which gives free veterinary care to pets owned by homeless people and other vulnerable groups affected by poverty, and Therapy Dogs, which brings together dogs and people – for example, it takes animals into nursing homes and hospices. I know this cheers people up because I saw my mother's reaction to a visit from a dog: some of her old spirit and love of animals suddenly flared up, despite her dementia. We should never underestimate the joy and love animals can bring us.

I'm always happy to attend Thirsk events and have been impressed by the talents of the town's knitters, the Yarnbombers. Just before the 2016 Tour de Yorkshire they put up hundreds, probably thousands, of woollen creations – around bus shelters, bollards and doorways, as well as shops, pubs and the Herriot centre. A statue of Alf was apparently made more eye-catching thanks to the addition of pink leg warmers. Hundreds of people of all ages were involved in the display, including a 97-year-old. I spotted knitted chickens, owls, sheep and cows, even Yorkshire puddings, plus knitted testicles attached with fasteners so that I – Mr Testicle is my nickname, remember – could remove them.

In 2016 Lin and I and around 350 others – including Jim and his sister Rosie, Donald's daughter Janet, and many Herriot fans – attended a black-tie dinner in Leyburn, organised by Ian Ashton from the Herriot museum. Now in his 70s, Ian was formerly an engineer, but he's done some fascinating things: running a falconry centre and breeding deer, ostriches and wild boar among them. I was once the official vet at a snail race he organised, probably the least taxing work I've ever done. Now Ian beavers away promoting Herriot and what he stood for. One of his many successes was the big celebration for what would have been Alf's 100th birthday. Ian wanted guests to remember his life and take part in a fundraising auction. While we all tucked into beef and Yorkshire puddings, around £3,000 was raised for the James Herriot Foundation Trust, set up to help youngsters who want a career in animal welfare. Jim and Rosie and actor Christopher Timothy gave speeches, and the singer Lesley Garrett performed. It was particularly enjoyable to see the cast of *All Creatures Great and Small* embrace one another on the red carpet, together again after more than 25 years. I was over the moon to finally meet the actor Robert Hardy, who'd played Siegfried (Donald) so brilliantly. He made a grand entrance, sweeping in last when everyone else was having pre-dinner drinks. The main doors suddenly flew open and there he was, his arms outstretched.

"Good evening!" he boomed, his voice strong despite his 90 years. He had a walking stick in one hand and was wearing a trilby hat, a white silk scarf and a dinner jacket.

Robert was much in demand that night, but I managed to get his autograph and have a chat. I explained that I'd worked for Donald for many years and had become a partner in his former practice. I also told him I thought his portrayal of Mr Sinclair was brilliant. Typically, Donald himself hadn't really liked it, but Robert already knew that. I was saddened when he died a few months later.

The centenary party gave us an excuse to reflect on Alf's life and death, not that I really needed any prodding: our lives had overlapped so much. For many years before his death he lived in Thirlby, not far from Donald and his magnificent hall. It's a tiny and beautiful village where Lin and I had built a house, although we moved on about a decade ago when we wanted a renovation project. After Alf retired we'd sometimes see him around Thirlby and have a chat, although we were never regular visitors to his home. He valued his time and especially enjoyed spending it with his children and grandchildren. Herriot fans sometimes arrived in the village looking for their favourite author, but often couldn't find him: locals would say, with puzzled expressions on their faces, that they had no idea where he lived, protecting his privacy because they liked and respected him. I knew Alf was grateful. As time went on I saw him very infrequently. He became increasingly frail and gaunt, his body finally losing its fight against cancer.

When I heard Alf had died in February 1995 I immediately walked up to his house, very upset. His family were devastated but stoical. Cancer is an evil disease, but at least there's often time to say goodbye. His daughter Rosie was a GP and, like vets, is used to dealing with death; but it's obviously different when the deceased is your father. Both Jim and Rosie were very close to Alf, but I remember her trying to console me that afternoon, despite her own grief.

"That's life," she said, gently. "We all have to go some time, Pete."

Alf's funeral was a family affair, but in October 1995, eight months after his death, there was a service to celebrate his life at York Minster. Around 2,300 people attended, including many friends and vets. Lin and I were there and found it an emotional but uplifting day. Particularly bittersweet was hearing a school brass band, which included one of Alf's granddaughters, playing the theme tune from the TV programme *All Creatures Great and Small*: it brought back so many memories, and I found myself looking back on a rural life that was fast disappearing. Of course, as Jim says, it's easy to think of the "good old days", but were they really so good? Despite the tough physical challenges of the job, I think they were, and I was at times overcome with emotion that day. But there were also smiles and laughter. Christopher Timothy and Robert Hardy read out Herriot extracts and excerpts from one of Alf's favourite comic authors, P.G. Wodehouse. I thought the fun was appropriate, given that Alf had really disliked funerals, finding them too solemn. I think he would have been chuffed to see people remembering him with such warmth and good cheer, but bemused at all the attention.

I sometimes find it difficult to reconcile the Alf Wight I'd known with James Herriot. It's hard to fathom just how much he did, albeit unwittingly, for Thirsk and Yorkshire. He was, in his own opinion, just doing his job as a vet and writing some stories, so when I see the tourism paraphernalia, it feels rather odd. Significantly helping Britain's travel industry in his own lifetime must have felt even odder to Alf. Now I wonder what he'd have made of the Herriot visitor attraction, which opened at Kirkgate in 1999, and its Herriot mugs, coasters and tins of sweets. What might he say about the bronze statue of him in the garden of his old practice, and of Robert

Hardy's brass plaque from the BBC TV series, with "S. Farnon, MRCVS" etched on it, being sold at auction for £2,700? He'd no doubt have found it bizarre.

It was certainly bizarre to see such a massive sea of faces in one of Britain's finest cathedrals, gathered in York because of the literary achievements of a simple husband, father and country vet. Of course, I'd read his books, and while I certainly enjoyed them, Alf was never Herriot to me. I felt as if I was at a memorial for two entirely different people: one a vet, the other a literary giant. My connection with Alf was through his work with animals. I had not been involved with his other self, apart from seeing the autograph-hunting fans at Kirkgate and occasionally meeting Christopher Timothy when he popped in. But what I saw in the minster that day was how much Alf the writer was celebrated and respected.

I was pleased to pay my respects, but mostly just glad to have known Alf. To me he was simply a man who'd taught me about looking after animals – and human nature. I learnt a lot of my bedside manner from him. Once he told me how, very early on in his career, before Thirsk, he'd gone out to calve a cow. The farmer had been trying unsuccessfully for more than an hour when Alf turned up and performed the task quickly and easily. He was very pleased with himself.

Later his boss asked him how it had gone and Alf said, "Very good. I had the calf out in no time."

The boss told him he'd made a mistake, because he had made the farmer look a fool. "You're a young lad. He won't think you've done a fantastic job; he'll just see you've made a bit of a fool out of him by doing it too easily. You're highly trained, but the farmer has a lifetime of experience. Don't make him look stupid."

It was clearly a lesson that Alf had taken to heart.

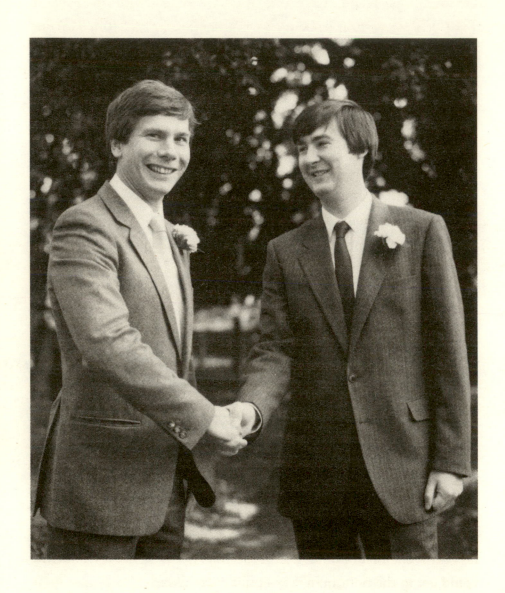

Mark Robinson, Peter's best friend and best man at his wedding.

CHAPTER 8

Saying Goodbye

As a vet dealing in life and death, I know that things do not always end well, but I still shudder when I look back to one particular day: 14 October 2009. It was the day my best mate Mark Robinson, who I'd met in 1976 on our first day at university, hanged himself. This fantastic friend and successful vet was 52.

In many respects, he was a happily married father of two and a devoted family man. Around 14 years previously, he had suffered from acute depression. It had lasted a couple of years before "the light switch came back on", as his widow Louise said in her written tribute at his memorial service. He was desperate to know why he'd been affected, but he was unable to put his finger on it. Something was clearly very wrong but, despite Mark's intelligence and analytical mind, he couldn't say exactly what it was. He told me he thought he had a chemical imbalance in his brain, and believed that if he could get to the bottom of it he could cure himself.

Devastatingly, that was not to be. That's the nature of mental health issues: so often they can't be easily explained or dealt with. Certainly, more needs to be done to stop so many people killing themselves. Between 2003 and 2013, more than 18,000 people with mental health problems took their own life in the UK, says the Mental Health Foundation. In comparison, the population of Thirsk is about 9,000. I think it's worth pointing out that this century, until 2017, just 126 people had been killed in the UK in terrorist attacks, according to the Global Terrorism Database. Terrorism is despicable; I myself was caught up in the London "attack" in 2017 that turned out to be a false alarm: a few of us were locked in a shoe shop until the so-called crisis was over. But in the UK, suicide is far more prevalent than terrorism. We should remember that when deciding what to worry about and how we should allocate resources.

Louise's own theory about Mark is that he was goodness personified, a Samaritan to all those in need, but often not to himself. "He saw good in everyone so when someone criticised or hurt him, it hurt him to the core," she wrote. "He found it difficult to cope with negativity of any sort."

Tragically, the light switch went off again, and then came the terrible day when Mark decided death was preferable to life. Louise is still furious that although Mark told his GP he had suicidal thoughts, she — his wife — wasn't informed because of patient confidentiality. Louise, who began dating Mark after our ridiculous attic stunt in Liverpool, decided two days after he died that from then on she'd do what she could to help the charity Mental Health Research UK. She's been a tireless campaigner for the organisation (then in its infancy) ever since. It's the UK's first charity dedicated to funding research into mental illness, and to developing better treatments with fewer side effects. Mark's memorial and a sponsored walk raised £30,000, which was donated to the charity — the first sum it was given. Since then it has gone from strength to strength, with

Louise and her family, friends and colleagues donating more than £100,000 down the years, often through sponsored cycling, canoeing and running events. Emma, one of Mark's daughters, raised £800 when she got married, asking for cash instead of wedding presents. Less than a decade after his death, donations in Mark's memory have funded many research projects, including one looking at online intervention to treat depression in university students.

Suicide is preventable, yet it's the biggest killer of men under 50, says secondary school teacher Louise, and the leading cause of death in young people and new mothers. Around 13 people kill themselves every day in England, with men most at risk. She knows what she's talking about; not long after Mark's suicide she became a member of the National Suicide Prevention Strategy Advisory Group and regularly travels from her Shropshire home to attend meetings at the Department of Health. She believes that breaching patient confidentiality should be allowed if there is a danger the patient could kill themselves. It could have saved Mark's life.

There has been some positive movement in recent years. There's a five-year plan in place to reduce the suicide rate in England by 10% by 2020, and new investment so more people can be treated in the community, something lacking when Mark was ill. Louise says GPs need more training about what to look out for. This determined and big-hearted woman is still grieving, but finds at least a few crumbs of comfort in her mission to prevent other people taking that final, desperate course of action. She is particularly pleased that depression in young people is now being taken more seriously. A recent study found that academic pressure, bereavement, bullying and alcohol or drug misuse contribute to many childhood suicides.

"It's good to see that mental health and emotional wellbeing are high up now on the school agenda," adds Louise, who wants them both to be compulsory subjects on the curriculum.

I still beat myself up wondering if I could have done more to help Mark. Louise sometimes talks about the "ripple effect" his suicide had on family and friends. When someone you love takes their own life, you are never quite the same. A heart attack or a car accident would have been bad enough, but suicide is a whole other thing. You feel guilty, and ask yourself certain questions over and over again. I often telephoned Mark, but should I have called him more? Should I have visited him more often? If I had, would it have changed the outcome? He often didn't want to talk about himself, but I knew things sometimes got to him. I remember he'd been upset about losing a client to a neighbouring practice. It happens to all vets, but can be like a dagger through the heart; many people with depression might hear 1,000 compliments, but only remember the single negative remark that comes their way. Should I (could I?) have done his job for a while so he could have gone on holiday, as Eddie Straiton did during Alf's depression? Should I have taken Mark on holiday? He worked very hard, as vets usually do, but he had plenty of holidays and was surrounded by people who adored him. Would taking him on yet another skiing or watersports trip have made any difference?

About two weeks before he died, in what was to be our last conversation, I told him I would visit soon. It was increasingly difficult to meet up because of work, family commitments and also distance, with me being in Yorkshire and him in Shropshire. I remembering him saying it would be nice for us to get together again. I will always regret not having a word with Tim and Julian, swapping a shift or two and getting in my car. But whether or not it would have changed what happened, who knows?

I do know, though, that suicide can happen to people you love, and to people who are successful. I can be a blunt Yorkshireman at times, and don't always find it easy to share my thoughts and feelings, but I hope Mark's death has helped me understand that some issues need to be shared. No one should ever think that "Bob" is not "the sort" to kill himself. Anyone could be "the sort" and everyone needs a helping hand. There should be no stigma attached to this. If you break your leg, you get help. A poorly mind should be taken as seriously and treated as sympathetically as a poorly body. We need to talk about our fears and worries with friends and families, as well as with the professionals if necessary, and find out much, much more about how society can prevent suicide.

Louise bravely came to a couple of university reunions after Mark's death, which we all found hard. He should have been there. Young people around the world go away to university and form close friendships; our "Attic Gang of Six" was just the same. When the remaining five get together, the first mention of his name usually makes us all well up. Then we often remember something he said or did that made us laugh. It cheers us up, at least for a bit. I will always miss him, a loyal and funny friend who always managed to see the other person's point of view, but I now try to cherish the good times. I hope Louise and her daughters can do the same.

Sadly, Mark is not the only person I've known to commit suicide. It's fairly common among farmers and vets. Recently the Farm

Safety Foundation revealed that more than one agricultural worker commits suicide each week. The suicide rate among vets is almost four times higher than the national average: a staggering 40% have thought about killing themselves. There's even a 24/7 helpline for vets, run by the charity Vetlife. Suppressing problems, limited financial gain, long hours and access to drugs are all said to be contributing factors to the suicide rate. I think many colleagues would see more than a grain of truth in that. For me, part of the problem is that vets have to make some big decisions. GPs can send their patients to hospital for further treatment, but vets mostly have to roll up their sleeves and get on with it. We make life-and-death decisions, which can be a heavy and lonely burden. The pressure can easily build up, and sometimes we have a run of bad luck.

Towards the end of Jim's veterinary career, I saw him at Skeldale one Monday morning after he'd worked the weekend. He looked miserable as he trudged in, his shoulders bowed. When I asked if he was all right he simply said, "Plenty of deaths, Wright. Plenty of deaths."

I knew exactly what he meant. This is a major downside of the job: not being able to save an animal, or knowing the kindest option is to end its life, can really get to you. And perhaps your private life is not going well or you have financial worries; vets are often self-employed, with the responsibility of running a practice and employing staff as well as treating animals. Factor in the ever-increasing expectations of pet owners and changes in treatments and medicines that vets need to keep on top of, and it's easy to see why many of us feel stressed.

I've already mentioned that I suffered from depression as a teenager, but although I've had periods as an adult where I've felt gloomy, they were a very long way from what Mark went through.

They were also far removed from Alf's breakdown. In diaries written when he was a student he'd talked about bouts of "the blues". Years later, his wife and children were so worried about him that they thought he might not recover. He even had electro-convulsive "shock" therapy, which passes small electric currents through the brain. Later, he became a Samaritan, giving callers the opportunity to confide in someone – something it seemed he himself hadn't done. I think anyone who happened to get Alf on the end of the phone was lucky; he wasn't at all judgemental, and was a really good listener.

If more people, particularly men, had been willing and able to bare their souls in his era, he probably wouldn't have suffered so much. It's so much easier now to talk about mental health problems. I only wish everyone could find a shoulder to lean on, somewhere they can share their worries.

Donald was a popular man and undoubtedly had shoulders to cry on, but he still took his own life at the end of June 1995, at the age of 84. Like Alf, he was a man in a man's world – and in Yorkshire, too, where men didn't (and often still don't) tend to share their feelings. Plus, some of the people he would have counted on, such as his friend and colleague Alf and his wife Audrey, had just passed away. Donald had had a stroke a few years previously, and while he'd recovered reasonably well (even flirting again with some of his female friends) he was not the same, and could no longer work. Donald rang Jim two or three days after Alf died in the February of that year. His calls had always been short and to the point, and this time he just said,

"Jim, I'm fed up about your dad!" before banging down the phone. It wasn't a throwaway comment. He was devastated.

Some of us knew that Donald had, for a long time, been in favour of voluntary euthanasia, a process that gives a person the option to die. They might ask for someone to help them die, refuse medical treatment or ask for it to be stopped, or stop eating. Although we were all very upset to hear the news, we weren't surprised when Donald took an overdose of pills, normally used to euthanase vicious dogs we couldn't get near. I'd heard him say a few times that people could start to think they were no longer useful; they could get to the point where they'd had enough of living. Joan Snelling was doing some paperwork for Donald in Kirkgate one day, many years before he died, and came across a few leaflets about the Voluntary Euthanasia Society, which was set up in the 1930s. She didn't comment, and filed the papers away.

After his wife died in the middle of June, I saw Donald drive past me a couple of times. Previously he'd have waved jauntily and stopped to chat, but now he just looked haunted, a sad figure slumped at the wheel; his sparkle, his own "light switch", appeared to have been turned off. He came into the practice about a week before he died and stood slouched against the radiator, his head down and shoulders forward. It was obvious he was deeply unhappy. He still had his big and beautiful home, but he was now on his own, with no family nearby; his son lived abroad and his daughter down south.

Donald is certainly not the only elderly person to commit suicide, or try to; it's more common than we might think. But as he'd been a vet, he was able to get his hands on lethal drugs that regular members of the public can't access. Joan bumped into her old boss in Thirsk's marketplace on what would turn out to be his last trip into town. He was very quiet and not himself but, of course, he had just been widowed. He told Joan he was fine. A few hours later he was in a coma. I was at work when Jim told me that Donald had taken some pills. It was a horrible few days, with Joan in floods of tears and all of us constantly asking how he was, although words seemed meaningless in the face of his condition. Jim kept us informed, but we knew Donald wouldn't get better and that it was just a matter of time before his organs packed up. He lingered for a few days before he finally passed away.

The Voluntary Euthanasia Society is now known as Dignity in Dying. Its focus is not on assisted suicide, but on assisted dying. The organisation says this gives a dying person the choice to control their own death if they decide their suffering is unbearable. Assisted dying is still illegal in the UK, but some people find the means to end their lives, including Donald. He got his own way in the end, as he usually did.

There are many emotional traumas lurking in a long life, and other difficult times lay ahead. In 2010, my world fell apart when Lin was diagnosed with cancer. It was August when she found a lump in her left breast. She was just 50. Her GP said it was probably an infection and prescribed antibiotics for a few days before referring her for tests. I was worried, but buried my head in the sand and focused on work, as I often do during difficult times. It's usually a good distraction. When I saw Lin's mammogram results, though, my heart sank into my boots. There was a hideous, obvious mass and I wished there and then that I hadn't been trained to read such results; ignorance can sometimes be bliss.

I went to pieces, although Lin was calm.

"What will be, will be," she said. "We'll cope. There's no point worrying."

The NHS was fantastic, before and after surgery and during chemotherapy. Lin was very brave and very positive. But I struggled. I was lucky I had good friends to talk to; I didn't want to stress Lin out with my worries. My daughter Emily had already moved out by then; Andrew was working, but still living at home. I didn't want either of them to know how frightened I was, but I expressed my fears to others and tried not to bottle things up. I sometimes telephoned Tim Parkinson, a farmer and lifelong friend whose wife had, not long before, had an operation to remove a brain tumour. I'd listened to him when he'd needed me, and here he was returning the favour, even though his wife was not out of the woods. I'd sometimes be driving somewhere for work, and my mind would wander off to Lin's cancer. Using the hands-free phone, I'd tearfully tell Tim I couldn't cope. He was a good listener and it was helpful to talk to someone who understood. Being a pessimist, I was convinced Lin would die.

Someone who cheered me up no end was one of my clients, Graham Bird. *Yorkshire Vet* viewers might remember this warm and friendly man. The only other non-female in his large family is a castrated donkey called Teddy, one of many animals on the Birds' smallholding. I arrived at Graham's place one day during Lin's treatment. He saw my face and asked me what the matter was. When I'd explained, he told me not to worry, threw in a couple of jokes and added: "Everything will be fine. Lin's a strong woman."

I came away smiling, as usual. I remember Graham telling me that he was once watching the programme with one of his granddaughters when she suddenly said, "I really like it when Peter's mother is on."

Graham told her my mother never featured on *The Yorkshire Vet*, but the little girl was insistent. He only realised what she meant when he saw me arrive at the Greens' farm in the next episode. Jeanie opened the door with the words: "Now son, how are yer?"

On her 51st birthday, a few weeks after finding the lump, Lin had a mastectomy. I was too nervous to sit waiting during the operation, so I returned to work. When I got back to the hospital later that day, Lin was groggy. She had medical tubes coming out of her and, of course, she had only one breast. But that didn't matter. She was alive, although we'd been told the cancer was an aggressive type that might have spread. More tests were needed.

I was still gloomy, having unwisely looked for medical opinions and statistics online, which only served to feed my pessimism. I now feared Lin might have no more than a few years left. Plus I knew a lot about various diseases and conditions; sometimes the ailments of humans and animals are similar. All can suffer from depression, dementia and cancer. I'd seen grief-stricken cats and prescribed them diazepam, and removed cancerous tissue from many animals, particularly dogs. I'd also carried out many mastectomies. With so many advances in veterinary medicine, I'd been treating more and more animals with chemotherapy and drugs designed to shrink tumours. Sometimes my efforts would fail and the animal would suffer even more, to the extent that I'd wished I hadn't bothered. Other times it all worked brilliantly. A couple of years ago, I discovered a lymphoma in a 10-year-old boxer called Arnie. He had other health problems too, but his owner was keen for me to start treatment. Chemotherapy for many months, medication and a healthier diet, including kale, seemed to do the trick, and the dog thrived with few side-effects. He hasn't had chemotherapy for more than a year now and still enjoys running around the woods. He has real quality to his life, which is what it's all about.

So the vet and scientist in me gave a clear picture of both the pros and the cons, but during Lin's treatment I tried to focus solely on the pros. She needed chemotherapy for several weeks and although Graham Bird was right – she was strong – she had to endure nausea and vomiting, and also the intense pain brought on by a cold cap, a special hat that freezes the scalp and can be worn during chemotherapy to try to prevent or reduce hair loss. Lin is very stubborn and didn't want to lose her crowning glory, so decided to give the hat a go, persevering with it until the end of her treatment. After each session she'd always have a smile on her face and say: "Let's get home. That's our sanctuary." Our dog Alf and cat Rosie would sit or lie by her side. Alf stopped asking for walks and often rested his head on Lin's lap. I'm positive both animals knew she was ill.

When the results came back and it was confirmed that Lin's cancer had not spread, I felt an overwhelming need to go to church. I do not push my religious beliefs onto anyone but I regularly attend services, and on this occasion I felt a real urge to thank God. I tried my usual church in Kilburn, but as it was getting late the door was locked; so I decided to drive to the peaceful church of my childhood, All Saints in Great Thirkleby, where my Granny and Grandad Duncalf helped out. Granny – loved by everyone who knew her – was often on her hands and knees there scrubbing the floor. I knew every nook and cranny, having run over there so often as a boy to help and, no doubt, to hinder. I always enjoyed watching Grandad ring the bells and often climbed up into the belfry with him. Sometimes I'd see him pumping the handle on the side of the organ to get it going; he lit the boiler the night before the Sunday service, walking alone through the pitch-black churchyard and descending into the basement – not scary for a man who'd fought in the first world war. He also cut the grass: he was a very precise man and it was always in perfect condition. As I stood there in the churchyard I could almost see my Grandad, working a scythe to keep everything tidy; only later on did he use a lawnmower. When his arthritis became really bad I would help by pulling an attached rope.

Like so many churches, this one has an alluring, tranquil air; it's small and serene, surrounded by fields – a perfect example of architecture and nature coming together in a harmony of stone, glass and grass, combined with tiles, flowers and trees. The churchyard is a haven for plants and wildlife. I enjoy strolling along the familiar footpath that runs through it and links up with many scenic walks, or visiting family graves: Grandad and Granny Duncalf and her sister Hilda (a heartbreaking 21 when she died in childbirth) are among several ancestors buried here. There's also my great-grandad Robert, Granny Duncalf's father and a talented stonemason. Somehow these links with the past helped me to come to terms with the life that Lin and I would now be allowed to enjoy together; a sense of calm descended on me after so many weeks spent wondering whether my wife would live or die.

Naturally, I still feared Lin's six-monthly, then annual, checks. She herself went through complicated reconstructive surgery and was not fazed by the check-ups. Then, towards the end of 2016, there was bad news: a mammogram taken at a mobile unit in Thirsk showed a potential problem and she was given an urgent appointment for an ultrasound scan in York. Here we go again, we thought, with Lin once more coping far better than me. I was due to inspect a riding school near Barnsley on the day of her test; I couldn't really put it off so I went along, although I fretted constantly as I checked the horses. By midday, when I hadn't heard from Lin, I was bracing myself for a devastating phone call. Later, she told me that when she'd seen her Thirsk mammogram with a big black circle around a particular area, she'd also feared the worst. But then, just as I was examining a horse's eye, my phone rang. I answered with more than a little trepidation, but immediately heard good news in Lin's voice. The consultant had said the scan had simply shown an enlarged but non-cancerous lymph node. I skipped out of the horse box full of the joys of spring, despite it being winter. The animal's owner must have thought I'd taken something in there that had transformed me into a raving lunatic. I was so happy.

When cancer touches people you love, it hits you like a sledgehammer. It tears families apart and Lin, the kids and I know we're lucky she survived. I somehow wanted to do something to acknowledge that, so when I was offered the chance to run a half-marathon for charity in New York over the St Patrick's Day weekend, I seized it. I could raise some money for cancer research and animal charities, I thought.

It all came about through my friend Bernie Slaven, a former Middlesbrough football player and radio presenter, and one of the team's best-ever strikers. I'd first met him when he moved into the area; I saw him out gardening one day and introduced myself as a big fan. It was over a curry that he told me he was going to run the 2013 New York half-marathon for diabetes research, and suggested I do it with him. By this point I was almost 56 and hated running if there was no ball involved, but I instantly agreed – even though Bernie was still fighting fit and four years younger than me. He was also a teetotaller who drank water while I sipped a pint. He told me we'd be joined on the run by Jonathan, a radio researcher in his 20s.

Despite my misgivings, which began a few hours after the curry, I began training a couple of times a week after work in the woods nearby. I wore old tracksuit bottoms and a battered T-shirt, plus a head torch, as it was often dark when I went out. I remember feeling worried I'd meet someone I knew or, perhaps worse, a stranger who might think I was a weirdo as I crashed my way through the branches, panting heavily. Soon I was running four times a week, two to three miles each time, timing myself. I was getting faster and my breathing was improving. When the bad weather set in that winter, I used my neighbour's running machine, although I hated exercising inside. But I saw all the sweat on my top and figured that the further the sweat travelled, the harder I'd worked. As soon as I could, I was outside again on a longer route than before – almost seven miles, which I could now do in about an hour and fifteen minutes. Sometimes I'd speak to Bernie on the phone. He'd moved house by then and said he wasn't doing much training. I told him I was too busy to do much either. I didn't want him to know I was trying really hard and then perform badly in New York; it was best he didn't know about my gruelling regime.

By this time, I had bought some expensive running shoes and was training with Paul, a postman who was older than me and had been a sergeant major in the army. His wife was Lin's friend and they'd decided he was the man to take me to the next level of fitness. He's a quiet, kind and decent guy but I sometimes thought he wanted to kill me, the regime was that brutal. He was like a machine – used to taking squaddies into the hills to train them. He also ran for pleasure. It was as if he lived to run. I didn't have his passion, but I too was beginning to enjoy myself and I was carried along by his enthusiasm. His encouraging words, breathing routines and the fact he was with me every step of the way helped spur me on through longer and longer routes, even if I was running on adrenaline by the time I got home. My belly disappeared, and I was fitter than I'd been in a long time.

Julian, who television viewers will know is a real Mr Fitness, had lent me a fancy exercise watch and told me that a time of about two hours for 13 miles would be fantastic. I wasn't there yet, but was beginning to feel like a professional when disaster hit, just a few weeks before the race. I developed tendonitis in both legs, and could hardly run. A sports physiotherapist put some special black tape on my legs, often used by real athletes, which helped, as did the painkillers. But although I was still able to use a cross trainer, for the last three weeks I couldn't run at all. I had to rest my ageing body. When we flew to New York on the Friday, I wasn't very chipper, wondering if all my efforts had been for nothing.

The five of us – Bernie, his partner Clare, Jonathan, Lin and

I – had a great day as tourists on the Saturday, including an atmospheric boat trip around Manhattan while it snowed. I'd been to the States, but never to New York, and gazed in awe at the Statue of Liberty and Brooklyn Bridge. I was, though, increasingly distracted by the thought of the race to come the next day, and irritable that evening as I tried and failed to find some pasta to eat, as advised by Paul the postman/trainer. Bernie, Clare and Jonathan wanted to eat something else, and as they were also in a different hotel, we said our goodbyes. Lin was getting cross about my obsessive quest for Italian cuisine, but I eventually found some. We managed to sleep for a few hours before getting up at 5am, so I could microwave some porridge oats.

I registered at around 6am, runner number 12,898 out of more than 15,000 participants. I didn't mind wearing a black bin bag on top of my flimsy running gear, like everyone else. We all looked silly, but the bags definitely helped keep the freezing conditions at bay. One minute I was jogging along to warm up, fiddling with Julian's watch and chatting to a few American runners, and then suddenly we were off; the race had begun and I wasn't even properly ready. I was near the back; Bernie and Jonathan were already well ahead of me – with the professionals, I thought miserably. Then I tried to rally myself. I was in New York and I should enjoy this, whatever the outcome.

At the first mile marker I thought I was doing badly; I'd spent too long fiddling with Julian's watch. I carried on, noticing runners getting high-energy drinks and throwing the empty bottles aside as they ran. When in Rome, I thought, grabbing one and doing the same. As we ran around Central Park I realised that some runners were whizzing by me. Soon, though, I began to see that

I was passing a few here and there – people who had previously sped past me. By the time I was on Fifth Avenue, heading towards Times Square, I was loving it. There were loud shouts from New Yorkers in the crowd: "You've got it! Go, go, go!"

I couldn't help but grin. As I ran past my hotel I spotted Lin and Clare, both calling out to me and laughing. This is awesome, I thought. Then I was at the Hudson River, where we had boarded the boat the day before. By the time I ran by Ground Zero, the site of the 9/11 attack, I remember thinking that if I never ran again, I'd never forget this experience.

The miles were now rushing by and although I couldn't seem to get any closer to an old man just ahead of me – he looked to be in his 70s – I was hurtling past many others. My race finally ended two hours, one minute and 34 seconds after I'd set off. I soon found out I'd beaten both Bernie and Jonathan by just a few minutes. I'd wanted to come in at under two hours, but at least I'd gone faster than my running mates – one of them a former professional footballer and the other about 30 years younger than me. My chest was puffed up with pride, although my feet and tendons were killing me. That evening, the three of us were sore; none of us were walking normally, but we were all on cloud nine.

Later, back home, we handed over several thousand pounds to charity, including a cheque to Yorkshire Cancer Research. The organisation says people in Yorkshire are more likely to get cancer, and more likely to die from it, than in most other counties in England. I don't know why that is, but since New York I've done several talks to increase awareness and have raised more funds to fight the disease. It's a noble cause and without all the dedicated people involved, my Lin would probably not be here now.

Although running the Big Apple was a thrilling experience, what sticks in my mind the most from that trip has nothing to do with the race. For some reason, we'd decided to take the subway and had headed underground. There we spotted a man busking. He was singing 'Oh Happy Day' – a well-known 1960s gospel arrangement of an old hymn – and Lin, who has a lovely voice and knows the song well, joined in. As I stood by watching while the pair of them smiled and sang, I felt an incredible wave of pride in my wife. She'd had to run her own race: against cancer. My bit of jogging was nothing in comparison.

Peter in the dispensary at his practice in Skeldale.

CHAPTER 9

Doing My Bit for Middlesbrough

The whole family loved Albert. This large, handsome pheasant would eat corn from our hands; sometimes we'd see a flash of colour and hear his croaking call, and then he'd start pecking on the window to show us he was hungry. He would strut across nearby fields to our garden, where we have a well-stocked bird table. We'd probably helped him survive three shooting seasons; no mean feat, considering a farmer regularly runs a shoot in and around the woods near our home.

We'd watched lots of pheasants pecking and running around over the years, but none were as friendly as Albert. We came to consider him a pet which was, in hindsight, quite naive, considering the high chance that we'd lose him. Pheasants have been killed for sport or food since the 19th century. Shooting is a popular royal pastime; a party led by King George V in 1913 was said to have shot more than 1,000 pheasants out of a "bag" of around 4,000. Millions of birds, reared for the sport, are released every year and are usually shot by hunters using dogs to flush them out. It's not everyone's idea of a good day out, of course, but it does create jobs and brings income into rural communities. Despite knowing that, we were still horrified when poor Albert died, although he did not meet his demise in the way we expected.

It was 2017 and I was outside painting a gate. Albert suddenly appeared and began strutting towards me from the other side of the road. I had no time to react when he stepped out just as a car was approaching. I closed my eyes and heard a thud. He didn't suffer, but I was upset and cross; the car had been going far too fast. Perhaps the driver, in his late 60s or early 70s, could have missed our beautiful bird if he hadn't been pelting along a country lane like a racing driver.

As he reversed he wound down his window. I could see he was shocked, but I couldn't help giving him a piece of my mind.

"You were going like a bat out of hell!" I snapped.

"I was only doing 40," he mumbled in a half-hearted apology.

He wasn't, and I told him in no uncertain terms to get out of my sight. He drove away.

Three weeks later I was busy at work, no longer thinking about Albert's untimely death, when I stepped into the waiting room at Skeldale. There was the driver sitting patiently with his border collie, right in front of me. As our eyes locked I don't know who was more embarrassed; my face reddened as I remembered the strong language I'd used in the heat of the moment. I quickly disappeared and asked a colleague to deal with the bird-killer and his pet. I managed to avoid them, realising that I'd perhaps overreacted when we'd first met.

Although Albert's death could have been avoided, it's sadly not an unusual fate for many creatures. I regularly spot the squashed remains of some poor animal on our roads, although I no longer see many hedgehogs. There are few of these iconic creatures now, so not nearly as many to run over. In early 2018 the *Guardian* said there were perhaps only a million left in Britain, down from an estimated 30 million in the 1950s. Then, to mark National Hedgehog Awareness Week 2018, writer and entertainer Pam Ayres published *The Last Hedgehog*, a book reminding us that unless we take action soon, the hedgehog will disappear.

Unfortunately, these spiky little mammals are not the only ones at risk of becoming roadkill. Vets are often called out to help animals injured by cars and lorries, including deer. Frequently, by the time they're found, they're exhausted as well as in great pain. We often have to put them down. Sometimes, though, wild creatures get into difficulties with not a road or vehicle in sight; I've known them to literally tie themselves up in knots in panic. I had a case not long ago, seen on *The Yorkshire Vet,* involving a deer that had become caught in the orange plastic twine used to wrap bales of straw. My friend Maurice, a retired farmer with about 40 hectares (100 acres), had called me out after finding him on his land. A deer expert, my neighbour John, accompanied Maurice and me as we raced to see the distressed creature. We took along a gun, just in case we needed to put him to sleep.

The deer had got himself tangled up on scrubland. Among piles of rotting manure there were also some reams of twine. The deer, about 18 months old, must have been foraging around and somehow got some of it wound around his antlers. As he tried to free himself, he twisted and turned, only succeeding in getting more tangled up. The plastic now resembled a rope about 5cm (2in) in diameter, some wrapped around his antlers and some wedged in the ground. He was anchored there and extremely distressed, as well as very lively: he was going crazy as he tried to break free.

A frightened deer is a dangerous deer; they might look angelic, but they have a ferocious kick and can use their antlers to nasty effect. They have even been known to kill a person. Bearing this in mind, we had taken a huge folded tarpaulin sheet with us and now stood behind it, knowing that if the deer kicked out, the sheet would give us some protection. We quickly threw it over the animal, then moved in and pinned him down so we could cut through the twine. He was frightened, but it only took a few minutes, and once he was freed we stood well back and watched him dart off at high speed. It was lovely to see, and lovely to know we'd probably saved his life. Maurice is fanatical about nature and really cares for the environment. He was angry that contractors who'd been spreading the manure had carelessly left the plastic twine on his land − a disaster waiting to happen, and one that could easily have been prevented.

The deer, despite everything, was far less tricky to deal with than Wendy the wallaby. I'd never handled a marsupial before; that much was clear to viewers watching *The Yorkshire Vet*, on which Wendy appeared. Monk Park Farm near Thirsk has hundreds of different kinds of animals, ranging from calves, guinea pigs and rabbits to deer, alpacas and wallabies, including Wendy. I'd been slightly apprehensive even before arriving at the farm, as I knew next to nothing about wallabies. If I'd been a vet in Australia the situation would no doubt have been different, but my career in Yorkshire had never lent itself to pouched animals with prominent hind legs. I can only imagine what Alf and Donald might have thought of my antics with this antipodean visitor, a species they almost certainly never worked with either.

Before I could treat her, though, I had to get hold of her. The kangaroo-like animal gave several of us the hop-around while our big orange net remained frustratingly empty. I'd been called out because she seemed off-colour – farm employee Paul told me that she was still eating, but getting thinner – but I remember thinking, as she sailed once more through the air beyond our grasp, that she couldn't be that ill. But when we finally cornered her, I could see that her coat was in poor condition. Something certainly wasn't right, although her heart sounded fine. Paul was worried that what-ever she had was infectious. As he and his colleagues held Wendy upside down with her tail in the air, I felt her stomach and found something strange – something solid. I wondered if it was a foreign body in her intestines, and decided an X-ray was needed.

The next day Wendy arrived at Skeldale in a cage in the back of a van, and was brought inside with a blanket over her head to help keep her calm. She looked like a prisoner who didn't want to be photographed entering court. I knew she'd hop quickly out of Thirsk given half the chance; so Rachel, our head nurse – who had also never dealt with a wallaby – sedated her, a mask on her face supplying the gas. Paul was on hand in case she panicked, but everything went smoothly.

The X-ray wasn't enlightening, and Rachel and I both frowned and muttered as we felt Wendy's tummy and looked at the photos of her insides. I still thought there could be a foreign body in there, but decided more research was needed on this wallaby enigma; so I did what many of us now do to find something out – I looked on the internet. Looking back, I perhaps should have done that in the first place, because I immediately saw that what I thought was an "alien" object was nothing of the sort: it was a pouch support bone. Of course! Silly old me. But that still begged the question: what *was* wrong with Wendy?

Picking up the phone, I called my old friend and housemate Andy Routh, one of the Liverpool "Attic Gang of Six". He used to be head vet at London Zoo and is now with the Durrell Wildlife Conservation Trust in Jersey, founded by the well-known author Gerald Durrell, who wrote *My Family and Other Animals* (since adapted for television). The trust's mission is to fight species extinction. I've been to visit Andy in Jersey and admire both him and the trust. Keeping animals in captivity is not as good as them living in the wild, but it does help us to learn about them and helps prevent them being wiped out. On the phone, I asked Andy to tell me a few things about wallabies, a creature he was familiar with. He suggested I check for an infectious disease called actinobacillosis. I did, but the blood tests came back negative.

In the end I found the solution myself. Another blood test had shown that Wendy's muscles were being affected by a nutritional deficiency. Her keepers had told me she often picked out the bits of food she liked and left the rest. I gave her a shot of antibiotics and some multivitamins and sent her home. When I saw her a week later she had put weight on and had a gleaming coat. She was so well it was hard to pick her out from the other wallabies. She bounded over a high fence at one point, as though powered by high-octane fuel. The episode was a reminder that as a vet you never stop learning – and never know what you might be called on to treat next.

There's a joke with more than a little truth in it that goes something like this: What do you call a vet who can cure only one species? Answer: a doctor. Just think of my colleagues and me, having to deal with the likes of Wendy the wallaby or the circus elephant, not to mention alpacas, baby emus, ferrets and geckos. Vets have experience with so many animals, especially mammals – many of which share a number of characteristics with humans, including warm blood and four-chambered hearts. They can feel pain, get cancer and flu and suffer from heart failure and diabetes. They can also have a whole host of other complaints that humans can relate to. Cats, for example, can be born with cerebellar hypoplasia, which has symptoms similar to human cerebral palsy. They too can live full and enjoyable lives, despite tremors and jerky movements. Pets also suffer from grief; just watch a dog or cat after the death of an animal they've been close to.

So it will perhaps come as no surprise if I say that my veterinary skills have sometimes come in handy with people. Occasionally, a farmer will ask me to take a look at an infected finger or treat a chest infection. Sometimes at the end of a farm visit I'll hear the words, "While you're 'ere, can you 'elp? I'm coughing up all this green stuff." Farmers don't always have time to visit a GP, especially in the spring when they're dealing with lambings and calvings day and night. I've given many of them antibiotics, as some are suitable for both humans and animals.

I'm certainly not the only vet to have treated people. Donald employed a man called Johnny Goldsborough who lived in an outbuilding next to his home. He planted and harvested Christmas trees, helped with the animals and looked after the grounds. One day he had excruciating toothache so he went to find Donald, who told him to take a seat and lean back. Before Johnny knew what was happening, his boss had pulled out the rotten tooth using a pair of pliers from the workshop. Another time, Donald offered to remove a cyst from a client's back, as he'd noticed her wincing with discomfort when she brought her pet in to Kirkgate. The woman told him she was already booked in to have the cyst removed by a doctor; but if she'd said yes to Donald, I'm sure he would have sprung into action.

On one occasion, in the 90s, I like to think I not only helped an injured person, but also did a favour for my football team, Middlesbrough. At the time, my daughter was friends with Jade, the daughter of the club's striker Paul Wilkinson. She'd often visit their nearby home, and I was a little starstruck, even envious, that she spent so much time with him and his teammates. I would happily have paid to sit there all day talking football with these professional players.

Often, when Emily came home from Paul's, I'd ask who else had been there.

"John was there today," she might tell me.

"Is he Scottish?"

"Yes," she'd say.

"That's John Hendrie, a fantastic winger and international player," I'd say wistfully, although it meant nothing to my little girl. To her the men were just other adults.

One day, though, I got to go round myself. It all started when Paul's wife rang to say that Paul had been cleaning out a drain when his leg had slipped into it, and he'd injured it. They'd left a message with the Middlesbrough club doctor, but hadn't heard back. She asked if I could help.

I quickly drove to their home and found Paul sitting with his leg up on a chair. He'd gashed his shin badly, taking off a lot of skin, and was bleeding. As a mucky drain had been involved, I was worried about infection. Fortunately, I had plenty of antiseptic in the car so I cleaned the wound religiously before putting on a sterile dressing. There was no need to bother with the club doctor after that. Paul's leg did very nicely, which was a relief; having a one-legged centre forward would have been bad news for me and every other Middlesbrough fan. If it had been an opposing team player, though, perhaps I'd have considered amputation.

Sadly, there was one occasion when my help proved useless. A couple in their 60s had brought their Labrador bitch into Skeldale to be put to sleep. I remember the man standing as his wife knelt beside the dog to console her in her last few moments. As I injected the lethal dose and the much-loved pet peacefully slipped away, the lady began leaning on me. At first I thought she'd fainted, but as she leaned further and further over I realised something was seriously wrong. Glancing at her face, I saw she was very pale; I thought she'd probably had a heart attack. Someone rang 999 and I started doing CPR. The lady stopped breathing several times. St John's Ambulance has a station nearby and its staff arrived quickly, followed soon after by paramedics and an ambulance. Unfortunately, the poor woman died shortly after being admitted to hospital. She'd had a massive brain haemorrhage. I felt so sad for her husband, and still do to this day. He lost both his wife and his dog within just a few hours.

I don't think anything I could have done would have made a

difference; it all happened so quickly. I believe, though, that there's a lot more room for vets and doctors to work together to save the lives of both humans and animals. It's an area Barbara Natterson-Horowitz, an American cardiologist treating humans, is passionate about exploring. She says human and animal medicine shouldn't be seen as separate fields, and she's made it her mission to try to close the gap between them. She's now the co-author of the bestselling book *Zoobiquity: What Animals Can Teach Us about Health and the Science of Healing*. The word "zoobiquity" combines *zoo*, derived from the Greek for "animal", and ubiquity, which means "everywhere". Doctor Barbara sounds like a fascinating individual and one worth listening to. She once told a newspaper: "There's fossil evidence in dinosaurs of stress fractures and gout. When I think gout, I think Henry the Eighth."

In 2014 she gave a TED talk (TED is a non-profit organisation that tries to spread ideas, often through short talks watched online by millions), in which she explained how she'd answered a phone call a few years before that changed her life. She was then a doctor specialising in cardiac imaging techniques and was asked to visit an elderly female chimpanzee in a Los Angeles zoo. The animal had woken up with a facial droop, and her vets were worried she'd had a stroke. They wanted the doctor to check her heart to see if there was a possible cardiac cause.

She was soon working with other animals, and began to see how similar they are to us. She described how she listened to a lion's heart after a life-saving operation to drain fluid from the sac in which the heart is contained. Doctor Barbara said the procedure, which she had done on many human patients, "was identical, with the exception of that paw and that tail". She began to question why she had never thought to ask a vet, or consult any veterinary literature, for insights into her human patients. "Why had I never, nor had any of my physician friends and colleagues whom I asked, ever attended a veterinary conference?"

Doctor Barbara also talks about the emotions animals display, and how they too are similar to those shown by humans. The Herriot books, all based on real events and characters, included a lovely tale about a pig called Nugent becoming a friend to Mrs Pumphrey and her Pekingese dog Tricki Woo, both of whom I've mentioned before. Nugent was treated very well by the wealthy animal lover and, as Herriot said, "It couldn't have happened to a nicer pig because, though most of his species have an unsuspected strain of friendliness, this was developed in Nugent to an extraordinary degree. He just liked people and over the next few months his character flowered under the constant personal contact with humans."

If we are this close to so many animals, both physically and emotionally, it's not a big jump to understanding Doctor Barbara's view that we can benefit from a fuller understanding of our shared biology. To quote just one of her colourful examples, she thinks knowing more about polycystic ovaries in a Holstein cow "can help us better take care of a dance instructor with painful periods".

Much of what Doctor Barbara advocates lies in the future. The past has to be left behind, and nothing illustrates this better than our move to a new practice. *Yorkshire Vet* viewers might remember an episode early on, where I visited my old place of work at Kirkgate – now the Herriot visitor attraction – and talked to a group of children about being a vet. Probably no one knew that on that day (and, indeed, on any day I walk through the building's red door) I felt a whole host of emotions – wistfulness and regret at the passage of time being among them. The day our practice left the building was perhaps one of my saddest.

We said goodbye to Kirkgate in the centre of Thirsk and moved to new premises on the outskirts of the town in 1996. It was difficult, but necessary. As with so many things in life, the veterinary world continues to change. Alf, for example, talked in his books about the disappearance of draught horses as the tractor took over the heavy duties of farm work. By the early 1990s, around the time my two bosses retired, farms were becoming bigger and fewer. Today Skeldale deals with only three dairy herds, but in the 1980s Kirkgate had around 60 on its books, many of them with just 10–20 cows, far fewer than on today's farms. Farmers used to know the names of all their animals, just as my friends the Greens still do. But as the farming side of our work started to decrease in the 1980s and 90s, the pet side of the practice began to expand. That meant many more clients coming into Kirkgate, which had hardly any parking facilities. This created problems, as it was hard for some people to walk far or lift poorly animals. We also began to realise that we needed more space for operations, consulting and equipment, such as scanners and up-to-date X-ray machines. It had become clear that Kirkgate was simply not up to the job, so in 1994 we reluctantly decided we'd have to find somewhere new.

It was only after Alf and Donald retired in 1990 that Jim, Tim and I became full partners. Four years earlier I'd become a salaried partner, which meant I received some of the profits but had no say in how the business was run. At that time I was preparing to get married, and made it clear I would leave Kirkgate if some kind of partnership wasn't on the cards. Both Alf and Jim had to apply some pressure before Donald finally relented. Then in 1990, after Donald's stroke, I moved another notch up the ladder. Being a full partner meant I could actually help move the practice forward, and had a real stake in its future. Despite initial misgivings about relinquishing control, Donald sent me a gracious letter thanking me for all my hard work.

A few years later, Jim, Tim and I were the ones who took the responsibility for deciding to move. Although Alf and Donald, now frail old men, no longer had a formal role, they still had their opinions. We welcomed them and always took them into consideration. Donald, predictably, was a little negative, partly as he owned Kirkgate and the business paid him rent. Plus, it had been his home for a period and his workplace for decades. All this meant he had a strong emotional attachment to it. Alf, too, had never been one for change and, like all of us, he loved Kirkgate and everything it stood for. Years before, he'd seen no need to buy new curtains for the office when Jim's wife Gill had criticised one particular pair; they must have been hanging there for at least 40 years. If he was reluctant to change something so small, imagine what he thought about moving completely. He also had far more important things going on in his life, not least his struggle with cancer. Eventually, though, he realised the move was both necessary and inevitable and gave us his blessing.

Once the decision had been made, we hit upon another problem: we couldn't find anywhere suitable, so in the end we decided to design and build our own surgery. We needed a site with planning permission that was accessible to clients, meaning lots of parking spaces. We talked to a few landowners but weren't making much headway, so we visited an industrial estate on York Road, heading out of Thirsk. There were still plenty of plots for sale. We realised that this was the perfect location, close to main roads and with plenty of space for us to build what we wanted. We'd be able to get out to calls quickly and clients would be able to visit without too much fuss. Excited, Jim, Tim and I went away with bits of paper and came up with designs to present to the architect.

I was, however, worried about money; my family had always drummed it into me not to borrow too much. There was also no asset to sell because Donald owned Kirkgate – whatever we chose to do would have to be affordable. Looking back, we should perhaps have made Skeldale a little bigger, but a bigger debt then seemed a terrifying thought. The practice had some savings, but not anything like enough to pay for the land and building work. While we pondered what to do at a time when interest rates were not nearly as low as they are now, Jim told us that Alf wanted to lend us the money, interest-free, to be paid back over ten years. I will never forget this generosity, especially as the offer came while Alf was very ill.

Unfortunately, neither he nor Donald lived to see the building completed, nor our move in to Skeldale. It was a great shame; I would love to have given them both the grand tour. I think they would have been impressed with everything, including our in-house laboratory, isolation ward and dental suite. Alf's widow, Joan, honoured the loan after her husband's death and we continued to pay back what we owed, initially to her and then to the family estate when she herself passed away. A few years later, Tim, Julian and I bought Jim out of the practice when he retired. Not long ago Jim told me that moving from Kirkgate had been sad, but the best thing we could have done – and he's right.

The day we moved – a Sunday in March 1996 – was understandably hectic. We had to rush, because we planned to open for business as usual the following day. Many relatives, friends and colleagues pitched in, including our children and secretary Joan Snelling. Marion Baldini, whose mother was Donald's housekeeper at Southwoods Hall, was also there; she's now Skeldale's efficient administrator with her own office upstairs. Her desk, brought from Kirkgate, originally belonged to Alf's mother-in-law. A couple of friends, Howard Metcalfe and Malcolm Watson, also helped; Malcolm worked in the clothing business and brought along his huge van. Like so many people who move, we underestimated just how much stuff we had to shift and how long it would take to shift it. We also came across some unexpected items. In Kirkgate's cellar we found about 30 bags of coal dust – goodness knows how long they'd been there.

Many other rediscovered items triggered memories, including old daybooks listing appointments and the vets allocated to carry them out. We couldn't resist stopping to look, and there were a few tears, as well as some laughter, as we flicked through. In one book (sadly, now lost) there was an entry relating to Donald visiting a budgie at an old people's home. He hadn't charged, the notes said, as the bird was dead by the time he got there. Donald's freebie visit had come on the very day he'd demanded a formal meeting with all his vets to discuss the money he was sure Kirkgate wasn't making: a concern that bordered on paranoia. I clearly remember us gathering at the practice after a really gruelling day, ready to hear more about the state of our finances.

As it turned out, Donald didn't even turn up. He'd gone home early. We then decided to look in the book to see exactly what he'd been doing that day to earn us money. The only entry for him was the trip to see the budgie; so while putting the screws on all of us, all he'd done was something for nothing. It was yet more evidence of Donald's inconsistency and eccentricity, but also his compassion.

We called our new home Skeldale after the name of the practice in the TV series *All Creatures Great and Small*. A few journalists were interested in the story of our move, and someone said it had even been announced on Radio 4 that the Herriot surgery was moving from a lovely Georgian house to an unlovely industrial estate. I didn't hear the piece myself, but it was said to have painted a picture of us moving to some kind of dark satanic mill that belched out smoke. I know Skeldale isn't as eye-catching as Kirkgate, but it's only on the other side of Thirsk. I chuckled at the media's exaggeration. If the reporters could have seen the medicines, paperwork and other veterinary paraphernalia that were already in place that first day, they would have known that we were as dedicated to doing our job as ever.

Of course, we didn't unpack everything immediately. Some boxes containing memorabilia wouldn't be unpacked for months. Many of those bits and pieces ultimately ended up in the old office cabinet I've mentioned, which now stands in the staffroom. As it turned out, the moving day was also a day of work; a lady brought her puppy in. Despite being busy, we couldn't turn her away. It was business as usual and our patients, as always, came first. Luckily, it wasn't anything severe and we were able to treat the little animal and continue with our mammoth task.

I can't remember much about driving away from Kirkgate as my workplace for the last time. I was too busy or, more likely, I was trying to suppress my emotions. It certainly hit me a few days later when I went back to pick up some boxes and saw the building stripped clean, its heart and soul gone. On that last Sunday I was simply focused on making sure Skeldale would be operational in a few hours. There was a little time, though, for a symbolic gesture. Kirkgate had once employed a veterinary assistant called John Crooks, who's mentioned in the Herriot books. John had worked with Alf and Donald before striking out on his own in Beverley in 1954. He took with him a medicine bottle full of "air" from Kirkgate and released it in his new practice to, as he put it, instil the same atmosphere and friendliness. In 1996 we did the same, opening a bottle of "Kirkgate air" inside Skeldale. It was a fitting tribute to the place we'd left. We all hoped the magic of the old practice would continue to work in our new home.

Peter and Lin with Prince Charles at St. James's Palace in the
wake of the 2001 foot-and-mouth outbreak.

CHAPTER 10

A Bottle of Wine from Prince Charles

I am in no doubt that I live in one of the most beautiful parts of England, maybe the world. It's not the Caribbean or the Amazon rainforest, but when I wake up and see the glorious Yorkshire countryside right outside my bedroom window, I feel like the luckiest man alive. Obviously, I'm not the only person who's had these thoughts. Turner, one of Britain's greatest artists, renowned as "the painter of light", came to Yorkshire for the first time in 1797 when he was just 22. The young man was inspired, returning several times to sketch and paint. He stayed for weeks at a time at Farnley Hall near Otley with his landowner friend and patron Walter Fawkes, a descendant of the infamous York-born gunpowder plotter, Guy Fawkes.

Just like today's tourists, Turner went to some truly magical places; his Yorkshire subjects included Malham Cove and Bolton Abbey, which he painstakingly captured for eternity. It's thought that around 1816 or so, he went to Rievaulx Abbey, Scarborough and also Sutton Bank where, more than 150 years later, I'd enjoy walking with Alf and his dogs. Turner made six double-page sketches of the area and experts believe he was planning an important treatment of it. However, there doesn't seem to be a finished Sutton Bank panorama: a shame, but no tragedy. The exquisite view is still there for all to see.

If I'm lucky to have Sutton Bank on my doorstep, I'm even luckier to have the wildlife. Owls are a particular favourite. A few years ago, I often saw a barn owl (a male, I think) swiftly and silently flying past my house at dusk. He was probably on hunting expeditions, and I soon began to look out for this oh-so-quiet assassin with his heart-shaped face. Sadly, he disappeared one winter following a heavy snowfall, his species yet another we are seeing less and less of. There are many reasons for this change, including the conversion into homes of old family farms and outbuildings, which are perfect for owls. Small mammals, the prey that owls feed on, are also disappearing, something that's linked to intensive farming and the disappearance of meadows and hedgerows. I've treated several barn owls for broken wings, as they often fly into electric cables. Sometimes I have to put them to sleep. I'd occasionally watch "mine" going in and out of a hole in a tree a mile or so away, hard at work trying to find supper for himself and, perhaps, for the female and babies nesting inside. Males often give female birds gifts of food during courtship, so I decided I'd do my bit for romance and the survival of the species by putting up an owl box.

I've had my box up on the shed for about four years now. Each night I put in dead chicks donated by local hatcheries, putting to good use food that would just be thrown away otherwise. Then I make my own version of an owl hoot, to let the birds know the food is there. I used to feel silly doing it, but it seems to do the trick. Sometimes they arrive so quickly I suspect they've been waiting for me. I regularly hear them at night, shrieking away in the woods nearby, and wonder if they "discuss" this strange human creature who feeds them.

The only disappointment I've had with my owl box is that it hasn't yet been used for nesting. I was therefore a little envious when Maurice (the retired farmer who'd found the deer with twine in its antlers) called me one Saturday morning as excited as a child on Christmas Eve. He had three owl boxes up; two of them were home to not-so-glamorous pigeons, but the third contained, in his words, "three little balls of fluff".

"Baby barn owls!" he exclaimed, his voice quivering with pleasure. "If I'd won a million on the lottery, I couldn't be happier." He was so thrilled at the thought of an owl – three of them, in fact. He wasn't exaggerating.

Like all vets, I often try to give Mother Nature a helping hand, but there have been occasions when there's been little I could do. The foot-and-mouth epidemic in 2001 was one of those times. It was a devastating period that saw the slaughter of millions of animals across the country in a desperate bid to prevent the disease spreading. It wasn't just a tragedy for the animals. It also ravaged our farming industry. I was at the centre of this storm, but could do little more than listen and advise. As the crisis went on, I became an ad hoc spokesman for farmers in my community whose world was turned upside down. I saw first-hand what carnage this hideous disease caused.

The epidemic came a few years after bovine spongiform enceph-alopathy, known as BSE or, more dramatically, mad cow disease. Dozens of people in the UK died from the human variant of BSE and millions of cattle were destroyed. Then came foot-and-mouth disease. It was first spotted in Britain in February 2001 by a young government vet checking a group of pigs due to be slaughtered at an Essex abattoir. He immediately informed the authorities, but that didn't stop the highly contagious virus (the most infectious I've ever seen) spreading like wildfire; indeed, it had already expanded into other areas as he made his frantic phone calls. Foot-and-mouth mostly affects cows, sheep and pigs. Although we didn't have many pigs around Thirsk (luckily, as pigs excel in passing on the virus) we did have an awful lot of cattle and sheep. The disease is airborne and can also be picked up through contact with an infected animal, perhaps in a market or during transportation from, say, a farm to an abattoir. The movement of animals is extremely common in the farming industry, so containing the virus was difficult. Animals can also be infected by contact with people. We can carry the virus in our nostrils, or on our clothing and footwear. Cars, lorries and tractors are other efficient carriers of the disease.

Britain hadn't had a foot-and-mouth outbreak since the late 1960s, but this attack hit the country with a crushing blow. It's not known for sure exactly how the virus arrived in Britain, but it could have started out in Asia and travelled here via South Africa, in catering waste or illegally imported meat. All we were concerned with at the time was how to contain it. Roads were closed, farms quarantined and the export, sale and movement of pigs, sheep and cattle were banned. Animals were shot and their bodies burned. More than 2,000 premises were infected and it took seven months for the disease to be eradicated. There were mammoth disinfectant efforts to try to stop people unwittingly carrying the disease on their jackets and wellies from one place to another. City residents were urged to stay away from rural areas and everyone was advised to keep off paths on farmland used by animals. Britain's several million anglers were asked to lay down their rods, and postmen had to drop off letters and parcels at farm gates instead of delivering them to farmhouse doors. Local and general elections were even postponed. Yorkshire really didn't feel like God's Own Country any more; more like a version of hell.

An animal fattened for human consumption then slaughtered for its meat is very different to an animal condemned to immediate death by the government. Many dairy herds had to be shot, as did calves and lambs. If healthy animals lived on farms or smallholdings next to infected ones, they too had to die – a ghastly process called contiguous culling. Overall, around 10,000 farms were affected. A lot of stock also had to be slaughtered for welfare reasons – if, for example, they didn't have enough space because they couldn't be moved. Some also died from the cold, as they couldn't be brought inside. Even now, I shudder when I hear a farm vehicle reversing with that familiar "beep beep beep" warning sound, remembering how JCBs would have to back up to load carcasses into huge leak-proof sealable lorries.

One of my oldest friends was a tenant farmer who was already in the financial doldrums when foot-and-mouth first struck. He flippantly told Lin he wished his animals could catch the disease, so he'd be compensated; there were tales of some farmers being given huge sums of money. Most genuinely didn't want that, though – they would rather have had healthy animals. Many knew the different personalities and quirks of all their stock, but this particular friend of mine had too many for that, with 300 or so "fattening" cattle and 500 sheep. About a month after he'd spoken to Lin the farm next to his was infected, so his animals had to die too. His entire stock were shot. At first, it seemed he'd got what he'd wished for. But then he turned up at my home with red eyes and told me he'd been crying for hours. "I feel empty," he said. There was little I could say to comfort him. The fact that he wasn't alone in his despair was no solace whatsoever.

I was living in the village of Thirlby then, at the foot of the Hambleton Hills, surrounded by farmland. A neighbour had around 60 sheep in a field. Like many farmers he had his favourites, often feeding them bananas and even chocolate bars. Like my old friend's stock, none of these sheep had the disease, but they had to be killed anyway because they were next door to an infected farm. Lin took our children away so they wouldn't see the pile of bodies. In fact, though, you only had to switch on the TV to see the same thing; our screens were full of images of giant bonfires and mass graves. Sometimes carcasses were left to rot for days, the stench overwhelming. One farmer I knew lost his small beef herd of about 50 animals. He only recently bought more, unable to face the task of starting again until now. No one who watched the crisis unfold can ever forget it; around 11,000 cattle and sheep were killed in and around Thirlby alone, partly because there were few arable fields that would have provided natural breaks and stopped the spread of the disease.

At Skeldale we initially continued our farm visits, but we were only allowed to do non-routine emergency work to avoid us carrying the virus from place to place. There weren't nearly enough government vets (there'd been too many cutbacks over the preceding years), so later on, we and other private practices were drafted in to check for signs of foot-and-mouth on behalf of the Ministry of Agriculture, Fisheries and Food; symptoms included blisters around the mouth.

Vets came from other parts of Britain too, even from abroad. They mostly worked hard and were paid well, but they rarely had local knowledge. I heard of some being sent back and forth across Yorkshire to visit farms. Many ended up crisscrossing widely, when it would have been safer – and quicker – to do their rounds in just one area. To my mind, this kind of bad planning surely helped the virus to spread. I had some personal experiences of poor management. One day a vet from the south of England arrived in Thirlby in a Rolls Royce with a government list of farms to check. He asked me for directions to "Mr Davison's" farm. I informed him the farmer had left a decade ago; the land was no longer being farmed and a young couple were living there with their children.

One small blessing was that we were never involved in the culling. There were government slaughtering "gangs" for that, trained to do the job quickly and efficiently. They shot each animal with a bolt into the brain. The army was brought in to dig graves, burn bodies and also occasionally do some of the killing, as there were simply too many animals for the gangs to deal with.

It wasn't just the killing that got to me, though, but the ruin of the years of work – sometimes a lifetime – that it takes to build up a herd. More than once I visited Gerald Turton and his pedigree shorthorn cattle at Upsall Castle near Thirsk. The herd, started in the early 1900s, is beautiful to behold. At one point, Gerald and I were worried about little red marks in some of the calves' mouths. We knew these could be a sign of foot-and-mouth, but the cows often nibbled thistles, so that was also a possible cause. If in doubt, the regional Ministry of Agriculture office in Leeds had to be brought in. Their team thankfully thought the thistles were responsible, but Gerald and I were both on tenterhooks until then.

As the death toll grew, so did the anger, frustration and depression of the farmers. Compensation didn't always come through quickly, and many had problems coping with the sheer magnitude of it all. Some killed themselves, although no one I knew did that. Some farmers decided to leave farming for good, while others went on to dust themselves off and start again, either rebuilding exactly what they had lost or diversifying into different areas of farming. But that was later. As the weeks passed, I lost count of the number of farmers that I either saw in tears or had crying down the phone. Many would ask me if I'd heard of any new cases; some wanted me to approach the Ministry of Agriculture on their behalf. But it wasn't always easy to get information out of government officials. I heard the words, "That's confidential," or, "We cannot release that information to you" far too many times.

I was fed up that the ministry didn't seem to listen to people like me, who were working on the ground. We not only had a wealth of detailed local knowledge and could have offered a lot of assistance, but also cared for the welfare of the animals and their owners: our clients and friends. But we were at times surrounded by a shining example of chaos. I became increasingly critical of how things were being handled around Thirsk, and saw how some farmers began to distrust the government. Occasionally, they even tried to stop ministry officials getting onto their land. I was particularly disappointed that ministers would not admit that they were ill prepared for an outbreak of a disease on this scale.

After goodness knows how many sleepless nights from anger, stress and worry, I snapped. I'd needed to visit a farm a few miles away in the village of Knayton, but I'd heard rumours of an outbreak there. When I called the ministry to check, they wouldn't confirm anything.

"Whose interest is this in?" I barked. "Surely we are way beyond client confidentiality."

Enough was enough. It was time to air my frustrations publicly, so the sister of a local farmer who worked for the BBC in York fixed up an interview. I went on air to say that people were on the edge, that no one really knew what was going on and that the government's handling of the crisis was atrocious. I said we needed solid information – immediately. I was quickly invited onto Radio 4's *Farming Today*, followed by *The World at One*, on both of which I said more of the same. I turned down TV requests, though. I didn't want to be seen complaining; being heard was enough. About a week or two later, the government brought in a retired vet to liaise between the Ministry of Agriculture's Leeds office and veterinary practices. He was a great help and we immediately began to get a lot more useful information. Around the same time, I heard that a couple of advisors to the prime minister of the day, Tony Blair, had travelled up to Yorkshire and met with key figures from the National Farmers' Union to discuss the handling of the epidemic. Weeks later, it was all over. The virus had finally run out of steam, defeated by the wholesale slaughter, movement controls and all the other biosecurity measures. Foot-and-mouth also disappeared as it reached land where crops were grown, with few animals to infect.

For me, however, discussions about the outbreak were not quite done. Not long afterwards, I found myself laughing with Prince Charles as a Welsh farmer told us about the compensation he'd received for the death of his daughter's three guinea pigs. The creatures had been slaughtered along with all his stock.

The prince seemed surprised. "Really? They were slaughtered?"

"Yes," said the farmer, a small, quiet man. "They gave me seven pounds' compensation for each of them."

"What was that for?" said Charles.

The farmer was suddenly lost for words, so I leaned over and said, "Meat value, sir."

I was joking, of course. But I wasn't really poking fun at the death of the guinea pigs, which wasn't a laughing matter. It was just that a few pounds' compensation for three innocuous little pets, when entire farming communities had been decimated in an emergency that had cost billions of pounds, was surely an occasion for a little black humour.

But how did I end up joking with the heir to the throne in St James's Palace in the first place? Prince Charles had possibly heard me on Radio 4; at any rate, he invited me and Lin, and about 200 others, to a lunch at the gorgeous Tudor palace in the heart of London. The invitation letter said the prince, a well-known countryside supporter, wanted to lift the spirits of some of those who'd had a difficult time. I felt honoured to be chosen, and accepted at once.

Lin and I travelled to the capital and then headed to the palace with two farming friends, who had also been invited. I couldn't believe I was there. It's such a magnificent building, much of it built in the 1500s when Henry VIII was on the throne, annoying, frightening – or executing – six wives. History oozes from its stones. I read that Elizabeth I was based at the palace during the crisis with the Spanish Armada; Oliver Cromwell, one of many to sign the death warrant of Charles I, later turned it into a barracks. Queen Victoria married Prince Albert there in 1840. I felt a little overawed as we were ushered through security and into vast and elaborate state rooms with magnificent staircases and giant pictures of famous historical figures on the walls.

Perhaps surprisingly, as he'd invited us to lunch, the prince didn't appear until after we'd eaten our three-course meal and drunk more than a few glasses of wine. But he did mingle afterwards, speaking to several couples, us included. His staff had clearly done their homework because he knew a fair bit about our work and personal lives. He knew we had a son and daughter; he asked if they would follow in my veterinary footsteps. He also wanted to know about my working day and my role in the practice. He knew there'd been issues in Thirsk, but he hoped things were improving.

I have always admired Prince Charles and his work with the Prince's Trust. He leads a privileged but demanding life and does an enormous amount of good helping disadvantaged youngsters and sticking up for rural areas.

After he'd made a short speech he disappeared, but we were allowed to stay a little longer and revel in our grand surroundings. A few of us had a wander around to get a better look; Lin and I even managed to come away with a souvenir. When we were about to leave, she asked a waiter for a wine label to put in her scrapbook. Instead, she was given an unopened bottle from Prince Charles' own Highgrove estate in Gloucestershire. She came out with it under her jacket, as though she'd just stolen it. We've still got it and have no plans to drink it.

🦆

Foot-and-mouth was the most challenging episode of my career, but not the only trying time. In 2003 I was a prosecution witness in a high-profile court case involving a major food fraud, with several barristers on both sides. The trial centred on one of Britain's most notorious meat scams, in which about 450 tonnes of unfit and diseased flesh were deliberately passed off as edible. Massive profits were made by a factory in Derbyshire, which sold the meat to catering firms supplying hospitals, schools, supermarkets and old people's homes. It was said to be more lucrative than drug dealing.

I'd been called to give evidence because Moorland Poultry in the village of Dalton, near Thirsk, a processing plant I'd worked at for 20 years, had been one of several British slaughterhouses unwittingly providing dead poultry to the rogue business. At the time, several veterinary practices in North Yorkshire were contracted by the government to make sure hygiene and welfare regulations were being obeyed at Moorland. Welfare was taken very seriously; a vet had to be on site every time the turkeys were slaughtered, a major operation. I was the vet in overall charge and was usually there a couple of times a week for four hours a session. About 20,000 birds were killed every week, even more in the build-up to Christmas. A very small number – about 60-80 a week – were already dead on arrival at our plant, and were therefore deemed unfit for human consumption. We had documentary evidence to show that these were taken away and used to breed maggots, but unfortunately that turned out not to have happened. Most ended up part of the Derbyshire fraud.

Moorland Poultry was duped, and no blame was levelled at either the plant or me. But I was called to court as an expert witness to explain the role of the vet and how slaughterhouses operated. I was expecting all the brilliant minds of the large defence team to question my exact role and perhaps make me look silly, so I was a little nervous beforehand. But as I waited in the corridor outside, a policeman saw my worried face and tried to put me at ease, telling me with a grin that a lot of the illegal meat had been bought by the police canteen. His attempt at humour calmed me, but it turned out my nerves were unfounded anyway; the barristers, in their element "on stage" in their black robes and white wigs, only asked me basic questions that I could easily answer.

Later, I found out more details of the case. Six men were jailed after being convicted of recycling condemned and rotting meat over a period of about six years. Bird carcasses that should have been used only on maggot farms or processed for pet food were instead prepared and packaged as fillets at a run-down, rat-infested factory. The jury heard that the building was partly open to the elements; some areas had standing water that was contaminated with sewage. The meat was bought for as little as £25 a tonne, but after processing was sold for as much as £1,792, an incredible profit. Some of the poultry that had died on its way to the slaughterhouses was diseased, suffering from conditions including septicaemia and the food-poisoning organism, E.coli. Ringleader Peter Roberts – also known as "Maggot Pete" – fled abroad before the trial began. Convicted in his absence of conspiracy to defraud and sentenced to six years in prison, he was only locked up after four years on the run. Journalists found him wealthy, suntanned and unrepentant in his new bungalow on the Mediterranean island of Cyprus. After the court case, which came not long after BSE and foot-and-mouth, regulations around meat hygiene were really tightened up and it became almost impossible to flout them.

Sadly, though, the case hammered home the fact that there will always be villains who break the rules, people who are prepared to take advantage for their own gain. Despite our laws, we will always need to be vigilant, particularly when it comes to our natural environment. We all need rural areas, whether for enjoyment or to produce food; but they need us, too, and it's vital we do more to protect our countryside. I don't mind saying that I'm worried. When I behold Yorkshire in all its glory on a sunny day it can seem there's nothing wrong; but there are problems, and not just ones related to animal welfare. There's not enough affordable housing, and public transport in some places is very poor. Down the years, many schools, pubs and post offices have been closed. It's also well known that the immense power of our supermarkets is pushing down prices for farm products. Dairy farmers have been hit particularly hard.

Litter, particularly the plastic strewn across our countryside, is another issue. Lin and I regularly pick up piles of it. Many other people, including bestselling American writer David Sedaris, do the same – he even has a bin lorry named after him. He was on Radio 4 this year with presenter Clare Balding. They chatted while he made his daily round, picking up litter near his home in rural Sussex. They walked two miles and filled six bin bags. It's no comfort at all to know I'm not the only one obsessed with discarded bottles, sandwich wrappers, McDonald's cartons, cans and coffee cups.

The natural world is in danger like never before. According to the Yorkshire Wildlife Trust, 60% of wildlife in the county is under threat of extinction, coming under pressure from the likes of development, changes in farming practices and climate change.

The iconic puffin, seen around Yorkshire's coastal cliffs during the summer months, is one species in decline. Others are the skylark, the humble sparrow and the water vole. It's not just 'exotic' creatures far away from our shores that are slowly disappearing. The trust points out that all but a tiny fraction of our lowland meadows have disappeared since the 1950s, and that many of the changes affecting wildlife have also damaged the services nature provides for us, such as reducing the flood risk and pollinating our fruit and crops. I know I'm not the only one who finds all this frightening and depressing, but I've come to understand that simply watching, worrying and whingeing isn't enough. To quote my Granny Duncalf again, "A little bit of help is worth a lot of pity."

I also have reason to worry about things closer to home. For several years now, Skeldale has found it difficult to recruit new staff. When Alf was starting out in his veterinary career in the 1940s, there were very few jobs but lots of applicants. Now there are lots of jobs that just aren't being filled. That's despite there being more veterinary graduates than ever before. When Alf qualified, he knew vets who offered their services in exchange for just their board and lodgings, they were that desperate to work. Not so now. One key reason for this is that the expectations of how we work have changed dramatically in recent decades, something that has hit veterinary practices particularly hard. Many young vets now want to work nine to five, five days a week, but that doesn't always suit our type of work. Cows and sheep inconveniently give birth at 2am, and dogs get bones lodged in their throats at 9pm. Many new vets don't want to be on call, or prefer to work with just one species. That simply cannot be accommodated in a practice like ours. And despite the years of study it takes to become a vet, many nowadays tend to work for just five years or so, largely because most of them are women who want to take a career break to have children. Some don't come back into the profession. While bringing up a child is a noble undertaking, it does present us with significant staffing problems.

Why are so many of today's vets women? There are several reasons, one being that young women tend to perform better than men academically, and exceptional grades are needed to study veterinary medicine. Furthermore, with the decrease in farm work, there's less need for physical brawn to deal with horses, sheep and cattle; and when vets do need to restrain fractious animals, they now have a far wider range of drugs in their armoury. It's all very different from Alf's day, when you'd more likely see a five-legged cat than a female vet, and different from my own youth too. When I was studying in the 1970s, about 75% of the veterinary intake was male, but that figure is now down to just 10%. It seems to be a similar picture elsewhere. At the Herriot museum recently, I chatted to a young Turkish visitor who told me she was training to be a vet in Turkey. Most of her classmates were female too, she said. It's good that the profession is opening up to everyone but, as I've said, it does create a few problems.

I can have far too gloomy a view of the future; quite often, though, things happen that put my dark thoughts into perspective – I'll see an act of pure kindness or meet someone admirable who gives me hope. Rose Dawson is one of those people; I always enjoy a trip to her smallholding in Thirsk. With her husband, John, this caring lady in her 60s spends a lot of her time and money looking after injured owls. It's another of Alf's legacies: it was his idea to set up the sanctuary in the first place. The Dawsons moved to their 8,000-sq metre (2-acre) home in 1986 and initially had just a few sheep, bought mainly to keep their grass trim. Alf often visited to treat them or help with lambings, and one day suggested Rose put up some aviaries, saying he could fill them up for her.

"It would be useful for me when I get injured owls in," he explained.

Luckily the Dawsons agreed, and now, all these years later, I still take birds to them myself. Rose, who grew up on a farm, vividly remembers the first bird given to her by Alf – Barney the barn owl. He had a broken wing, which the vet had done his best to repair with pins. Barney wouldn't have been able to survive in the wild but lived happily in Rose's spacious garden aviary for more than 25 years. That's phenomenal. The Barn Owl Trust says a typical lifespan for a wild adult barn owl is just four years; the British record is 15 years. Alf and the Dawsons did Barney a big favour. It might not have been the life nature originally intended, but he was fed well and lived in very pleasant surroundings. He also had company for a long time in the form of Betty, a beautiful female owl.

Rose has pointed out that not all owl "injuries" are physical. The birds can have mental health issues, too, if they aren't looked after properly in captivity. Author J.K. Rowling certainly never wanted Harry Potter fans to read about the wizard's letter-delivering pet owl Hedwig, then go out and buy an owl. Unfortunately, that has happened, even though most people have little idea how to look after one. Some have to be rescued from rabbit hutches, garden sheds and greenhouses, tight spaces that give the owls no room to fly around.

Luckily, some rescued owls have been rehoused with the Dawsons. These days the couple regularly have more than 40 at their sanctuary at any one time. Many are eventually released, but the Dawsons continue to provide a home for those that wouldn't survive on their own. They've helped buzzards and kestrels, too, and also rescue other creatures including rabbits, chickens and goats. Donations, egg sales and money from their bed and breakfast helps fund the £600 or so they spend on the animals' food each month. There are many problems facing the countryside, but with people like the Dawsons there's just a chance my pessimism is a little overdone.

Peter with his Granny Duncalf on Scarborough Sands.

Percy Adds Perspective

Many of us find change difficult, but it can't always be avoided; we simply have to adjust. We learn to adapt to schools, classmates and teachers. We move house, sometimes even countries. We change jobs, get married and have children. We deal with divorce, illness and bereavement, and have to engage with new kinds of food and technology. Change is everywhere, but can still be difficult to accept. I'm in my 60s and often wish the idyllic rural life I enjoyed as a child, similar in so many ways to the world described in the Herriot books, still existed. But it mostly doesn't, although I often think I'd like to put the clock back. I'd love to see my parents young again. I'd love to meet up with my grandparents and have one more game of whist with Granny Duncalf in the village hall, then mow the churchyard grass with my Grandad. Of course, I know I'm sometimes guilty of wearing rose-tinted spectacles. I do realise that while change is often unwelcome, it can make things better; we do sometimes improve on the past.

Not long ago I had to grapple with an issue that went to the heart of everything I stand for. We were approached by a large veterinary company, a corporation that I would usually want to avoid, which offered to buy part of the practice. Over the last few years I've done many talks, usually for charity, and I naturally include anecdotes about working with Alf and Donald at the "Herriot" practice in Kirkgate. Its charm lay partly in its size: it was small and anchored firmly in the area in which it operated. Both Alf and Donald would have wanted to keep it that way. But in the end, Skeldale decided to sell a stake in the business.

So why did I change my mind? It certainly didn't happen overnight. It was one of the hardest decisions I've ever had to make, to let go of something so precious. I've worked at Kirkgate, then Skeldale (essentially the same practice) since 1982. I am very aware of my many responsibilities, and had to take into consideration the wellbeing of staff, patients and clients. I'm also constantly mindful of my duty to protect and continue the Herriot ethos.

The saga began in October 2016, when a firm of solicitors in London sent me (the senior partner) a letter saying the multimillion-pound company Medivet was interested in buying into Skeldale. It wasn't the first time such enquiries had been made; we'd been contacted by other organisations, too. For years, large firms have been swallowing up small veterinary practices. This kind of thing happens in many sectors – just think of supermarkets and farming – but Skeldale had always dismissed such approaches, preferring to keep doing things our way and keep full control. We believed that was best for us, best for our clients and best for our patients. We had occasionally talked to big organisations – sometimes even met their representatives – but that was as far as we'd ever got.

So when we agreed in early 2017 to meet Medivet chief executive Arnold Levy and his second-in-command John Smithers – both of them experienced vets as well as businessmen – we didn't see it as significant at first. We just felt we had nothing to lose in hearing what they had to say. I was expecting a chat and coffee before we went our separate ways; there was no reason to think the firm would be any different to the others we'd talked to. I picked up Arnold and John and their briefcases from Thirsk railway station (Medivet's headquarters is in Watford, near London) and made polite small talk while I drove them to the Golden Fleece, one of my old watering holes, where we were due to meet Tim and Julian, Skeldale's other partners.

This pub, opposite Thirsk's Victorian clock in the marketplace, has been a part of my life since I was a teenager. It was a major coaching inn before cars and trains arrived on the scene, in a time when people usually didn't go anywhere – if they did, they either walked or went by horse-drawn carriage. After the railway came to Thirsk, tourists started arriving and many stayed in The Golden Fleece. It provided good food, drink and a warm bed, even to the likes of great authors such as Sir Arthur Conan Doyle. So it was the perfect venue for our business meeting with Medivet, full of history and atmosphere (even if it does now serve Pornstar Martinis and cafe lattes). As Arnold, John and I walked in on that cold winter's day, I saw all the old black and white photographs of Thirsk on the walls and drew a little comfort from them. I was ready and willing to hear what Arnold and John had to say, but at first I was disinclined to accept anything they had to offer. They've probably had a wasted trip, I thought, and immediately felt a little guilty.

But there were problems within the veterinary profession that affected Skeldale, which is why we'd been willing to meet Medivet in the first place. Difficulties recruiting new vets was one big issue, a problem I've already mentioned; if you can't get enough staff, it puts a lot of pressure on the existing workforce. Old Father Time had made that an even more pressing problem. When we started negotiations with Medivet, Julian was only in his 40s, but Tim and I were a couple of decades further on. It's getting harder to haul ourselves out of bed in the morning or in the middle of the night, a problem that only increases with age, even though we never like to let a client down.

There was another problem too. Tim, Julian and I still enjoyed visiting farms and treating pets, but we increasingly found ourselves bogged down with paperwork and bureaucracy. There are so many rules and regulations covering the modern veterinary world now. It's mind-blowing. Jim and I often laugh when we remember a piece of sterilising equipment we used in the 1980s. It was nothing very technical, just a pressure cooker bought from the Army & Navy Store. At one point, it began making strange noises. As it hissed and crackled, we didn't dare get too close because we were worried it would explode. We would stand in the doorway of the operating theatre, then lean forward to flick the gadget's switch off with a broom handle. It sounds quaint and funny, but it would never happen in this day and age; health and safety regulations, rightly, wouldn't allow it. Perhaps that's one example of change for the better.

Furthermore, pet owners nowadays increasingly expect perfect outcomes, partly encouraged by improvements to medicines, procedures and equipment. The threat of litigation from upset clients is ever present. But vets, like all other human beings, do occasionally make mistakes; that's one of the ways we learn. Jim likes to tell the story of a vet called Hughie Begg who taught Alf when he was a student in Glasgow in the 1930s. Hughie used to say to the class: "You'll never make veterinary surgeons until every

one of you has filled a 15-hectare (40-acre) field with carcasses."
Obviously an exaggeration, but the point is clear.

Tim was waiting in the Golden Fleece when we arrived; Julian
wasn't there and it wasn't clear when he'd be free to join us, so we
started without him. During a few minutes of chit-chat over coffee
we learnt that when Arnold invited John to join Medivet, he'd
given him some advice: "Come and work for me," he'd said, "but
leave your ego on the other side of the door. You are very welcome
then." I really liked the sound of that, and instinctively began to
warm to both men. They then began asking about life at Skeldale.
Tim is usually quiet, so he left most of the talking to me. When we
began discussing our philosophies and what's important to us, my
ears really started to prick up; I was hearing things I hadn't heard
before from a big business. It was obvious that staff and clients
were extremely important to Arnold and John – it wasn't all about
money and profits. I told them about opening a bottle of Kirkgate
air when we moved to Skeldale in 1996, wanting to maintain the
practice's wonderful character, and they seemed to understand
why that was important. We'd always tried our best to modernise
while simultaneously maintaining the same level of friendliness and
approachability. "I think we succeeded," I told them. "But it's vital
to keep that spirit alive."

The two men were good listeners; they were no doubt good vets,
I remember thinking. I realised we all had a lot in common. They
were clearly concerned with doing the right thing for everyone and
liked what they knew about Skeldale, information they'd partly
gleaned from watching *The Yorkshire Vet*. They thought we'd fit well
into their company, explaining how their practices maintain a large
degree of autonomy. The firm's business includes nine 24-hour

centres, or hubs, based across Britain, all with state-of-the-art facilities. They also have a network of over 200 smaller veterinary practices, not open all the time but usually supported by one of the 24-hour centres. They promised that should we join them, they would let Skeldale take charge of day-to-day affairs. Head office would deal with a lot of the paperwork and keep us up to speed with regulations. There'd be economies of scale in buying supplies, including medicines, with hopefully some cost savings passed on to customers. There'd be a department to sort out vehicle problems and someone to find us a locum if we needed extra hands. Skeldale's vets could basically get on with what they did best: treating animals.

This was music to our ears. We wanted to – needed to, for our own peace of mind – secure the future of Skeldale. We had an eye on the time, already on the horizon, when we would retire. On the other hand, we didn't want the practice we loved gobbled up by a corporate giant that would trample over our unique way of working. By the time we'd finished talking, I was starting to think that perhaps these were people we'd be happy to go into partnership with. What they said made a lot of sense.

The four of us left the Golden Fleece and drove to Skeldale so Arnold and John could meet Julian and take a look at the practice. A little later, they were on the train back to London, ready to work out figures that they would present to us at a second meeting. I spent the intervening period talking to a few firms already working with Medivet. They told me they were happy and had very little interference from head office. I became convinced it was the right thing to do, and Tim came to the same conclusion.

Sadly, though, after some to-ing and fro-ing, Julian couldn't be persuaded. Tim and I begged him to give Medivet a try, even for a few months. The three of us had worked well together for 20 years; if he didn't like the new set-up, we reasoned, he could leave after that. But it wasn't to be. We bought him out of the practice and just before Christmas 2017 he left for pastures new. Afterwards, he told the *Times* newspaper he went because he was concerned the new regime would undermine the Herriot tradition; he was worried it would all be about financial targets. I think he's wrong, but we're all entitled to our opinion.

Julian wasn't the only one at Skeldale to be unhappy about our involvement with Medivet. We told the staff during a special meeting that included Medivet representatives, and there were a few tears and worries about the future. It was hard to put all these concerned minds at rest at this first meeting, because they hadn't spoken to Medivet as I had. Other staff, though, have found the whole process no bother at all. Now the dust has had time to settle, I'd say we barely notice Medivet's involvement. The company has been both hands-off and concerned about getting the big decisions right, such as which new vets to recruit. What would Alf and Donald have said of these changes? If they were around now, I don't think they would have been happy, at first. But they both understood that time does not stand still, and we all have to adapt to changing circumstances. Donald, who took over the Kirkgate business in the 1930s, had to seek work where he could find it. In those early days, quite a bit of the practice's income came from testing animals for tuberculosis. Alf even did some testing during his honeymoon in the Yorkshire Dales. Later, Donald made Alf a partner and then brought in Jim before Tim and I got involved. I think they would, in the final reck-oning, have understood the complicated and changing nature of the veterinary world and come to see that Tim and I, in good faith, had made the best decision for Skeldale.

The decision to sell or not was, as I've said, enormous. For weeks I'd felt I was carrying a huge weight on my shoulders. But the joy of my job is that there's always something to take your mind off things, always something to remind you that life has its lighter moments – and maybe those are just as important as the bigger ones. I was brought back to my everyday world by a simple peacock who went by the name of Percy and who turned up one day in the village of Dalton, near Thirsk.

Named by local children, this gorgeous blue, gold and green bird appeared suddenly. No one in Dalton seemed to know where Percy had come from, or why he'd chosen to grace them with his presence. Most people found him mesmerising, especially when he showed off his tail, and they enjoyed feeding him. But some residents found him a nuisance. He defecated on nicely manicured gardens and in the early morning would screech from the tops of walls and roofs. That's all well and good when trying to ward off tigers in Asia or to attract a mate, but it doesn't go down well with folk who've set their alarm clocks for 7am, only to be woken hours before. Percy no doubt made a stressful day at work a little more difficult.

Inevitably, a love-hate relationship developed between Percy and the villagers. But no one wanted it to end as it had the year before in the village of Thimbleby, 15 miles from Dalton. Pat the peacock was reported to have disappeared at the sound of a gunshot. Feathers were discovered at the base of a tree. No one was ever charged; peacocks are not covered by UK wildlife protection laws, as they are not indigenous birds. But there was a lot of anger over Pat's apparent death and fingers were pointed. Yet another peacock, called Peter (are there any Yorkshire peacocks whose names don't begin with a P?) also proved an annoyance in a village near Harrogate. He would peck at cars and damage paintwork, perhaps unsettled by his own reflection. A couple of years ago locals raised £500 to send him to a sanctuary. Last time I heard, though, he hadn't gone and was still poking around gardens and strutting along paths. He even had his own Facebook page.

When I received a call asking for my help in catching Percy, I immediately agreed, anxious to move him to a more rural location as soon as possible. Many people would miss him, but ultimately he would be happier. Peacocks can be aggressive and have sharp spurs on their feet; it could just be a matter of time before he caused a nasty injury. I had no real idea what I was letting myself in for, even though I'd caught peacocks before; a friend had asked me to find new homes for his birds when he moved house. I'd found out then that if you grab the tail feathers, they come out in your hand, so at least I knew I needed a better plan in Dalton. I arrived with a net and my son's old quilt from the airing cupboard, as well as backup in the form of my friend Mike. He has a smallholding with several peacocks and peahens and had agreed to take Percy home when we caught him.

We spent some time creeping through gardens like a couple of prowlers. Who needs theatre when Mike and I are around? When we finally found the peacock it was clear he didn't suffer fools gladly. I knew these birds could run at up to 10 miles an hour, but it felt as if Percy was going much faster. It had been a while since my half-marathon in New York and I'd forgotten to bring my running shoes, but as I pelted across lawns and pavements my net remained empty. Villagers thoroughly enjoyed the spectacle of Mike and me rushing around, shouting instructions breathlessly to one another; some obligingly helped out with "peacock" calls. But Percy would suddenly flutter up into the air, then land on a high wall or roof, in plain sight but out of reach, before hopping down into another garden. He was far more agile than us. The *Yorkshire Vet* camera was filming our every move and the crew were loving every second. For 20 years, I'd travelled to Dalton every week to visit the turkey slaughterhouse mentioned earlier: a respected and well-known figure here. Now I was little more than a laughing stock. Peter 0, Percy 1, I thought dejectedly as Mike and I left after two hours, deciding we'd have to come back the next day. "We will prevail," I said, rather unconvincingly.

When I went back I took along something similar to the concoction used by my old boss Donald to "stupefy" pigeons; given just a taste of it, birds very quickly zonked out. The drug I took was a more modern version, and was bound to work on Percy, I reasoned, as I confidently sprinkled some powder on a piece of bread and butter. Percy appeared and gobbled it all up while Mike and I sat in a kitchen for half an hour, sipping tea and watching through a window, waiting impatiently for the peacock to fall asleep. Another half an hour later I was sick of sipping tea and sick of watching Percy. He's not strutting, I thought – he's swaggering. Those watching seemed to be losing faith in my abilities; I could see curtains twitching. The pressure on me was building, and wasn't helped by the sight of the cameraman's shoulders shaking with laughter.

With fresh determination, I grabbed my son's old quilt and again ventured outside. Percy eyed me with disdain as he flew up with a squawk and landed on a chimney breast. There he wobbled slightly and fell asleep on his perch. The drug had finally worked, but the dastardly peacock was now out of reach. I wanted to swear out loud, but knew I'd be bleeped out for TV so merely said, "Oh dear, that's spoilt it."

I wanted the ground to swallow me up. What use was I? There was a building site nearby so, thinking on my feet and wanting to preserve what remained of my dignity, I asked the foreman if I could use one of his lifting devices to get to Percy and grab him before he woke up. But of course, health and safety rules put paid to that. I was defeated; Percy had won Round 2.

But victory comes to he who waits with an old duvet, or something like that. Before long I was back and this time I had more success, thanks mainly to a resident who'd intelligently enticed Percy into a garage with a trail of bread. The bird was finally cornered, and Mike and I just had to slip the net over him. My cheeks were still burning when we drove away with Percy's head peeping out from inside the tightly wrapped duvet.

At Mike's smallholding a few miles away, Percy was fastened up for a week or two to get him used to his new home, before being set free to make friends with a harem of peahens who'd been eagerly awaiting his release. He mated with one immediately, unperturbed by the cameras that were still filming him. He's now as happy as a pig in, well, you know, the brown stuff, which actually sums up me and my life. Sometimes things are tough and don't work out as expected, and sometimes we have to make difficult decisions. But I'm never happier than when I'm up to my elbows in muck, trying to improve the lot of all God's creatures. That's the life of a Yorkshire vet: a joy and a privilege.

Acknowledgements

My thanks to Helen Leavey, who eloquently put everything together and to whom I had to bare my soul.

Commissioning Editor Simon Raikes and Ben Frow, Head of Channel 5, whose original vision became a reality in *The Yorkshire Vet.*

Greg Barnett, our Commissioning Editor, who has driven the vision forward, guiding and supporting the programme.

Melanie Darlaston and Tony Moulsdale of Motion Content Group, who backed the making of *The Yorkshire Vet.*

Paul Stead, MD of Daisybeck Studios, who had the wonderful skills and artistic ability to bring the vision of *The Yorkshire Vet* to our screens. A man true to his word and who will be a friend forever.

Series Editor, Lou Cowmeadow, whose passion for the show has shaped the programme and has been pivotal in its success.

David Terry and the rest of the Daisybeck team based at Skeldale who I have had the pleasure to work with for the last three years. They have shown outstanding professionalism, empathy and attention to detail in capturing my work as a vet.

Thanks must also go to the talented Backroom Staff at the studios, who work tirelessly and receive no limelight.

Thank you to Amanda Stocks, of Exclusive Press & Publicity Ltd, publicist to *The Yorkshire Vet* and me – her wisdom and guidance in matters of which I know so very little has been invaluable.

A massive thank you to each and every one of my dedicated and hard working staff at Skeldale, without whom none of this would have been possible.

Thank you also to the wonderful clients of Skeldale Veterinary Centre who have embraced the *Yorkshire Vet* concept and participated in its making.

Thanks must also go to the people of Thirsk, of which I am one, who have welcomed and embraced *The Yorkshire Vet*.

Thank you to Jim Wight, my former Practice Partner and friend, who has helped mould my career, giving practical and common sense advice throughout.

A big thank you also to Jim's sister, Rosie Page, who has unfailingly supported *The Yorkshire Vet* from the very beginning.

Thank you also to Ian Ashton, who has been instrumental in making the World of James Herriot visitor attraction (which was our Veterinary Practice in Thirsk until 1996) the success it is today.

Thank you to Tim Yates, my colleague and latterly Practice Partner for over 30 years. One of the best, most hard working and unassuming vets you could ever meet – but even more importantly, one of the nicest.

Thank you to my lifelong friends from Liverpool University, Andrew Routh, Stephen Spencer and Nick Winn, who have contributed material and input where my memory was a little hazy.

A special mention also to Louise Robinson, wife of my dearest friend Mark, who is so badly missed by all who knew him.

Thank you to Heather Corner, an inspirational teacher who

ACKNOWLEDGEMENTS

shaped my early years at primary school, Joan Snelling, secretary to my bosses and mentors Sinclair and Wight (Farnon and Herriot) who kept me in line as a young vet, and Jackie Wilkinson, a close friend to Donald Sinclair, whose photographs and reminiscences brought a smile to my face.

Also a big thank you to Jo Sollis at Mirror Books, who felt that what I had to say about my life was worthy of print.

Thank you to my family, my daughter Emily, my son Andrew and my dear grandson Archie, who always brings me back to what really matters in life. Thank you also to my dear brother David, who advised and reminded me of parts of my life going back to my early childhood.

Peter

HELEN LEAVEY BIOGRAPHY

Helen Leavey has been a journalist for 20 years and worked for the BBC in London and Taiwan. She lived for a decade in China, where she tried her best to multi-task, as mum, journalist and Mandarin student, as well as holding down a job in human rights. Her love of the environment came into sharp focus in Beijing, where clean air, trees and grass were all too rare. Helen is a southerner, born and brought up in Slough, long before its already unsavoury reputation nose-dived with *The Office*. She now enjoys life in the North with her husband, a Yorkshireman who's been able to explain some of his county's more unusual words and traditions. They have two children.

ACKNOWLEDGEMENTS

Thanks to Peter and Lin for being such a pleasure to talk to, and thanks to the Greens, Heather Corner, Jim Wight and Joan Snelling for being generous with their time, anecdotes and photos. Thanks also to Micky, for having my back as always.

Helen